People-Centric Skills

People-Centric Skills

Interpersonal and Communication Skills for Financial Professionals

Second Edition

DANNY M. GOLDBERG

WILEY

Edition History
John Wiley & Sons, Inc. (1e, 2014)

Published by John Wiley & Sons, Inc., Hoboken, New Jersey.
Published simultaneously in Canada.

For general information on our other products and services or for technical support, please contact our Customer Care Department within the United States at (800) 762–2974, outside the United States at (317) 572–3993 or fax (317) 572–4002.

Wiley publishes in a variety of print and electronic formats and by print-on-demand. Some material included with standard print versions of this book may not be included in e-books or in print-on-demand. If this book refers to media such as a CD or DVD that is not included in the version you purchased, you may download this material at http://booksupport.wiley.com. For more information about Wiley products, visit www.wiley.com.

Library of Congress Cataloging-in-Publication Data

Names: Goldberg, Danny M., 1975- author.
Title: People-centric skills : interpersonal and communication skills for financial professionals / Danny M. Goldberg.
Description: Second edition. | Hoboken, New Jersey : Wiley, [2020] | Includes bibliographical references and index.
Identifiers: LCCN 2020008262 (print) | LCCN 2020008263 (ebook) | ISBN 9781119669302 (paperback) | ISBN 9781119669333 (adobe pdf) | ISBN 9781119669319 (epub)
Subjects: LCSH: Communication in organizations. | Interpersonal communication. | Auditor-client relationships. | Conflict management. | Problem solving. | Corporate culture.
Classification: LCC HD30.3 .G63 2020 (print) | LCC HD30.3 (ebook) | DDC 658.4/095—dc23
LC record available at https://lccn.loc.gov/2020008262
LC ebook record available at https://lccn.loc.gov/2020008263

Cover Design: Wiley
Cover Image: © Zach Dobson Photography

Printed in the United States of America

10 9 8 7 6 5 4 3 2 1

To my kids, Caleb and Liora, who continue to inspire and amaze me and are becoming great communicators in their own right.

Contents

Foreword

OVER THE COURSE of my 40-plus years in the internal auditing profession, I've had the privilege of meeting thousands of practitioners from around the world whose personalities are as varied and fascinating as their cultures. My experiences provide ample evidence to dispel an unfair and lingering stereotype that internal auditors are, well, dull.

Another typecast paints all internal auditors as shy and awkward introverts. I must admit (sheepishly) that one of my favorite jokes about internal auditing plays on this stereotype:

Q: Did you hear about the extroverted internal auditor?
A: He looks at your shoes when he talks to you.

But this, too, is an unfair and inaccurate portrayal. So why does it persist?

Part of the answer lies in the kind of work we do and how we do it. The only interaction many people have with internal auditors is fraught with concern.

Oh no! Why is our department being audited? What is internal audit looking for? Why are they poking around my records? Did I do something wrong?

With such tension as a backdrop to the internal auditor walking in the door, first impressions with our engagement clients go a long way toward establishing how they perceive our profession. If a team of auditors comes in the door with a no-nonsense and standoffish attitude, demanding records and pontificating about independence and objectivity, the lasting impression will not be a positive one. This is why building our soft skills—those skills that help us connect on a personal level—is critical to our success.

People-Centric Skills: Interpersonal and Communication Skills for Financial Professionals, 2nd edition, goes a long way toward getting us there.

I have known Danny M. Goldberg for many years. He has dedicated much of his career to championing our profession and helping practitioners build critical soft skills. For more than two decades, Danny has built and led internal audit functions. He is a well-known author in the profession and has published numerous articles in trade magazines over the years.

In this revised edition, Danny picks up where his 2014 book of the same name left off. He provides clever anecdotal teaching moments through his lead character, Dalton Zimmer, that focus on how auditors can approach different situations and scenarios. From interview techniques and reading body language to understanding the art of listening, the book covers important soft-skill topics, including self-awareness and empathy, emotional intelligence, and influencing change. His new book also provides an important update about communicating with two generations whose influence is growing quickly in business—Generation X and Millennials.

As a consistently eloquent voice promoting the value of effective communication, Danny reminds us that we must connect with people. That is why his first book resonated so well, and I'm certain that version 2.0 will, as well.

Richard F. Chambers, CIA, QIAL, CGAP, CCSA, CRMA
President and CEO
The Institute of Internal Auditors

Preface

PEOPLE-CENTRIC SKILLS:*Interpersonal and Communication Skills for Financial Professionals*, 2nd edition, is the follow-up to the 2014 critically acclaimed first edition. This first edition has been as rated as one of the top 30 interpersonal communication books of all time (bookauthority.org). The second edition aims to dive deeper into the critical skills necessary to be successful in the corporate world. Study after study supports the premise that soft skills are as important—or even more so—than experience or qualifications:

- According to a new survey of more than 2,000 adults conducted online by the Harris Poll, having soft skills—such as personal, communications, and time-management skills; enthusiasm; dependability; and reliability—without the required experience seems to be more desirable than having the right experience or qualifications for a job but lacking soft skills.[1]

- A 2018 study examined the views of hundreds of recent graduates from the **CEMS** Master in International Management program and over half (56%) consider either social skills (33%) or the ability to manage people (23%) as the most important skills to develop as technology increases in the corporate workplace. They rated these soft skills higher than teachable hard skills (7%), technical job-specific content skills (7%), or process skills such as critical thinking (12%).[2]

- LinkedIn's 2018 Workforce Report highlights a significant mismatch between the skill sets of today's top talent and the skill sets companies are seeking that LinkedIn CEO Jeff Weiner calls a significant skills gap.

---

[1] https://hrexecutive.com/are-soft-skills-more-important-than-the-right-qualifications/
[2] https://www.fenews.co.uk/featured-article/17062-are-soft-skills-more-important-than-education

"Somewhat surprisingly," Weiner says in an interview with CNBC, "interpersonal skills is where we're seeing the biggest imbalance. Communications is the number one skills gap."[3]

This is the easy-to-read story of a dynamic executive coach and trainer and the numerous clients he serves. Time and time again, our main character, Dalton Zimmer, is thrust into situations that emphasize the importance of People-Centric Skills. The book carries forward many of the skills highlighted in the first edition and continues to demonstrate the impact that interpersonal and communication skills—whether good or bad—have on a person's effectiveness, personal relationships, job, and career. Readers will be able to empathize with the characters and real-life situations highlighted in the book.

Topics include:

- Body Language
- Neurolinguistic Programming
- Gesture Clusters
- Facial Expressions
- STARS Method for Thinking on Your Feet
- Responding to Difficult Questions
- Reading Verbal Tone
- Emotional Intelligence
- Employee Motivation
- Self-Reflection
- Self-Awareness
- Emotional Intelligence
- Mode of Communication
- Change Management
- Transparent Communication
- Continuous Communication
- Public Speaking
- Voice Inflection

Our story takes us through the trials and tribulations of Dalton Zimmer, a well-known speaker and executive coach. Readers are led through many different challenging scenarios that test Dalton's resilience and character. Dalton

---

[3] https://www.forbes.com/sites/nazbeheshti/2018/09/24/are-hard-skills-or-soft-skills-more-important-to-be-an-effective-leader/#5e1f9a512eb3

balances his client demands with operating his business and attempting to be a good father to two kids, Caleb (12) and Liora (11). Some of the scenarios and topics covered in the forthcoming narrative include:

- **Chapter 1: The People-Centric Journey Begins Anew**: This chapter re-establishes our characters and sets up our storylines for the duration of the novel.
- **Chapter 2: Reading Through People**: Dalton arrives at his client (Sojo Technologies) in San Francisco to assist the CFO in interviewing a suspected harasser and fraudster, Julianne Cranson. Julianne is a high-level sales executive who has always been one of the company's top producers but is suspected of numerous violations, including kickbacks, undocumented discounts to customers, fraudulent reporting of travel expense, and threatening employees. Dalton advises and assists Kelli Jackson on how to approach Julianne and how to read her. Dalton has also coached Kelli on presenting to the audit committee and board and is planning a return visit for hands-on instruction for her team.
- **Chapter 3: Emotional Intelligence**: Dalton drives into San Jose to meet with Stanton Electronics Chief Financial Officer Brad Lester, a long-term friend and client. Dalton has his kids fly up and spend the weekend with Brad and his kids. Dalton takes in Dax's (Brad's eight-year old) soccer game, where Brad is an outspoken fan and parent. Brad is very demanding and vocal. After the game, Dalton and Brad talk about his impact on his son and how, in certain situations, Brad is intimidating without realizing it. The conversation dovetails into the importance of empathy and how to use it effectively to build relationships and relate to people.
- **Chapter 4: Different Points of View: Using Self-Awareness and Empathy Effectively**: The next day, after Dalton's deep-dive conversation with Brad on emotional intelligence and how to apply it in the workplace and at home, Brad applies these key learnings in an important conversation with his son, Dax.
- **Chapter 5: Wrong Mode = Wrong Mood: Determining the Optimal Mode of Communication**: Dalton's ex-wife is Caleb's newly appointed soccer team manager and wants to make sure the communication issues that the team has suffered from in the past do not continue to occur. Over dinner, Leslie and Dalton discuss some situations that have occurred and how they should have been communicated.
- **Chapter 6: Influencing Change Throughout Any Business**: Dalton delivers one of his signature courses on how to look for deficiencies

and continually improve any business process. Dalton starts the presentation with the importance of communication throughout any organization, highlighting the foundational keys to a successful corporate culture transparent, continuous communication.

- **Chapter 7: Projecting the Real You: Public Speaking**: Dalton meets another visit to the Bay Area to see Kelli and her team and discuss presentation skills and leading practices on how to deliver a compelling message.
- **Chapter 8: Coaching and Mentoring**: Dalton meets with Austin, head of Information Technology at Sojo Technologies, to determine the right path and approach to deliver feedback to one of his directors, David Allison. Austin is struggling with David because he was recently promoted to vice president, a role David believes should have been his.
- **Chapter 9: Presentation Skills and Body Language**: Dalton reviews the videos completed by Kelli's team and delivers feedback to the team on presentation skills and body language and other topics that assist in delivering a top-notch presentation.
- **Chapter 10: Thinking Quickly on Your Feet**: Dalton discusses leading practices in listening techniques and how to recall a person's name. He also discusses how the senior team might handle people who display aggressive techniques. He introduces the STARS method for thinking quickly on your feet, and how anyone can use it effectively.
- **Chapter 11: Coaching and Mentoring, Revisited**: Dalton previously coached Austin and assists him in delivering feedback to David Allison, a direct report he has struggled with since Austin's promotion to vice president. Dalton helps Austin deliver delicate feedback to make sure he and David are aligned moving forward.
- **Chapter 12: Crisis Management**: Prior to catching a flight, Dalton discusses the pros and cons of various ways to handle crisis management with Sojo CEO Brandon and CFO Kelli.
- **Epilogue**: We wrap up some of our storylines and find out what happens to Dalton, Lauren, Julianne, and others.

Acknowledgments

WANT TO THANK Tali Ploetz for her contributions to this book. With her vast experience in audit and risk, Tali wrote Chapter 2, which was critical to setting up our storylines.

I also want to thank the many people I have met throughout the years that have unknowingly inspired the stories in this book. Without you, the stories would only be fictional tales.

People-Centric Skills

CHAPTER ONE

The People-Centric Journey Begins Anew

 INTRODUCTION

Dalton finally settles into his seat on American Airlines flight 330, now delayed for three hours due to . . . who knows what the excuse is today. As a too-frequent traveler (and someone who loves control), he has given up on attempting to comprehend many things he cannot control. Happy to get an upgraded seat, he prepares for takeoff by gulping down a Tito's and soda, not taking the time to savor the flavor (or lack thereof). Regardless of the fact that he travels close to 200,000 miles a year, he never seems to get used to being on a plane—and out of a position of control. He very rarely sleeps in transit, so he plans to use his plane time wisely and goes through his running (and never-ending) task list.

At times, Dalton has overextended himself, even if he controls his own schedule. He fights a constant battle between having quality time and earning the money that enables him to have quality time. Tonight, he is heading from Sacramento to Orlando, but due to delays, he is routing through Miami and not directly to Walt Disney World. Instead of landing at the originally scheduled time of 5:00 am, this gets him in at 10:30 am—definitely a challenge to speaking coherently to an audience of 450 risk professionals at 1:00 pm. He has always viewed problems like these as self-imposed challenges and had fun with the circumstances.

One of the reasons Dalton took on this ambitious schedule is that it will give him the opportunity to meet his kids, Caleb and Liora, in Orlando and take them on a late summer trip to Disney World. The kids flew in with his ex; after a few years of getting a feel for their after-marriage relationship, he and his ex have achieved a very good rapport. In fact, it is reminiscent of the relationship he fell in love with. Revisionist historian—no regrets. Move forward.

Both Caleb and Liora have been accepted into a great middle school after suffering from constant bullying over the previous year. Fingers crossed, but everyone agrees this is the place both can thrive. This trip is a reward for all they have been through over the previous year.

Loving his job/company/profession Is key to Dalton's continued self-motivation. Keeping clients happy, making a difference, giving other like-minded individuals opportunities to be successful—this is what he lives for! Regardless of not sleeping for 32 hours, he known that when it Is his time to own the stage, he will always be successful, but maybe the time has come to avoid these kinds of scenarios! Over the past five years, Dalton's business has grown exponentially. His biggest hurdle—leveraging a business dependent upon one person/one personality—has been overcome by finding like-minded people and on selling clients not on a replacement for Dalton but on a different approach. All the other life coaches/trainers working with Dalton bring exceptional diversity in background and experience to the table. It works, but finding like-minded people was not a simple task.

This in-flight evening was slated to be full of administrative tasks: proposals, billing, client follow-up, and brainstorming strategies for client issues and potential go-to market strategies for some new initiatives. After takeoff (and turning on *Avengers: Endgame*), Dalton pops out his new rose gold tinted MacBook Air. Everything tech-related that Dalton owns is Apple and rose gold; he enjoys the general theme without explicitly stating that everything his team does turns to gold.

Dalton needs the noise of the movie streaming through his wireless headphones to help him block out distractions and focus more. After handling some of the mindless administrative tasks, Dalton turns to his detailed task list and begins to project-plan his approach to his new and continuing client engagements:

- For a new client in San Francisco, SoJo Technologies, Dalton has been called in by the chief financial officer, Kelli Jackson, to assist in interviewing a suspected fraudster, Julianne Cranson. Julianne is a high-level sales executive who has always been one of the company's top producers but is suspected of numerous violations, including kickbacks and undocumented discounts to customers, fraudulent reporting of travel expenses, and threatening employees. Kelli wants to handle this internally with some help. They have not been able to find evidence of fraud and are hoping a discussion with Julianne will resolve this one way or the other. Kelli and Dalton have been professional acquaintances and friends for a few years now. Dalton has also coached Kelli on presenting to her company's audit committee and board, and he is returning for hands-on instruction with her and her executive team. This meeting is scheduled for early next week, after the short jaunt to Disney World.

- Dalton is planning a visit to San Jose to meet with Chief Financial Officer Brad Lester of Stanton Electronics, a long time friend and client. During a quick phone chat, Brad mentioned some of the issues he has with his team and that they are not as dedicated as his previous teams. Brad is a workaholic, dedicated primarily to his job and secondarily to his family, and he expects the same from his employees.
- Dalton is also working with a new client in his hometown of Dallas on change management and driving cultural change.

If only all the issues on his plate were work-related (and therefore billable) rather than his day-to day life:

- Dalton's ex-wife, Leslie, is Caleb's newly appointed soccer team manager and wants to make sure the communication issues the team has suffered from in the past do not continue to occur. Dalton and Leslie are planning to discuss this during this weekend trip.
- Dalton is also working on a new project with his kids, highlighting the issues both have experienced through bullying over the past year. These are very difficult lessons for the kids but it's also a great opportunity to learn and, even better, help fight this very serious issue in all schools, specifically private schools.

Dalton's company has grown immensely and he is now just trying to keep up with the many moving pieces. More important, he's trying to be a good dad and role model to his kids.

CHAPTER TWO

Reading Through People

D ALTON ARRIVES AT the office of his client SoJo Technologies in San Francisco to assist the CFO in interviewing a suspected harasser and fraudster, Julianne Cranson. Julianne is a high-level sales executive who has always been one of the company's top producers but is suspected of numerous violations, including kickbacks, undocumented discounts to customers, fraudulent reporting of travel expense, and threatening employees. Dalton advises Kelli Jackson on how to approach Julianne and how to read her. Dalton has also coached Kelli on presenting to the audit committee and board and is planning a return visit for hands-on instruction for her team.

 ## PEOPLE-CENTRIC SKILLS IN THIS CHAPTER

- Differences between audit interviews and fraud interviews
- Fraud interview techniques and questions
- Reading body language, tone, and voice inflection in any situation
- Listening and responding to plausible deniability

KEY WORDS

- Reading People
- Body Language

- Neurolinguistic Eye Cues
- Gesture Clusters
- Facial Expressions
- Plausible Deniability

Another day, another long flight. Orlando to San Francisco is a nice six-hour jaunt and, on a Sunday night, is not exciting. Dalton loves to travel inconspicuously and not say a word to anyone throughout the flight. This is his me time. Draped in his Adidas Firebird tracksuit (reminiscent of Run DMC), he boarded for the long trip. He was sad to leave the kids with Leslie; he always is. It never gets any easier. It only seems to get harder on the kids, and that is why Dalton continues to rely more and more on his team. Early retirement is definitely the plan.

Once the plane settled into a comfortable cruising altitude, Dalton dove into researching SoJo Technologies. Kelli has been a friend for many years and Dalton has watched her grow into this role with SoJo. He always knew she was going to be a star; it was just a matter of time. She has been CFO for the past four years and the company has grown exponentially in that time. She has been a major part of the expansion and going public. Since before Kelli's arrival, SoJo's top salesperson has been Julianne Cranson. Julianne was one of the first employees of the company and has strong ties to SoJo's founders. She is one of the main reasons why SoJo has gone public and has grown over the past five years.

Julianne's profile reads like that of many top salespeople:

- Early 40s
- Extroverted personality
- Good conversationalist
- Always thinking five steps ahead
- Very good at psychoanalysis

Julianne will be a challenge for Dalton. She has been accused of rampant fraud, but the company has struggled to pin down the exact nature of the fraud. In fact, Dalton doubts if the owners really want to accuse her of fraud. She has been such a big part of the company's success that it is hard to think of SoJo without her. Jules (as she likes being called) has been accused of giving away software modules outside of the contract terms and other internal abuses. She has always had leeway to do what it takes to get the deal done. However, the leeway has turned into abuse, Kelli suspects. Jules has also been going through a bad divorce over the past two years: cheating, custody battle, a little bit of everything. Since the divorce proceedings began, Jules has been inconsistent. You could see it was taking its toll on her and her work.

When the long flight finally landed, Dalton hurried to the hotel to unpack and relax for a few minutes before calling it a night. There would definitely be a long day ahead.

The next day, as he summoned an Uber, Dalton shook his head as he thought about all the poor saps looking for a place to leave their cars while they dashed inside stores or restaurants for whatever brought them to San Francisco's Financial District. As his Uber turned onto Sacramento Street, he reflected on the fact that parking always seemed to be a challenge. What a beautiful day, with weather he rarely experiences living in Dallas. The bay wind whipped over his freshly shaved head as he headed for the elevator. His thoughts turned toward the day's visit to SoJo Technologies, the tech giant recently in the news for their latest medical invention, a device purported to eliminate the need for corrective lenses. Their product was expected to revolutionize the industry—no more surgeries, no more contact lenses, no more eyeglasses. Ever the skeptic, Dalton wondered if something like this could really work. The video showed users wearing the device at the office, in the gym, and while driving. *Well*, he thought, *at least it's stylish*. The promo ran through his head again. For as little as 30 minutes a day, you could eliminate the need for glasses? *Hmm*. If it worked, their device would cost a lot of people their jobs. He sighed. Therein lay the rub. Market disrupters are great until the layoffs start happening. Dalton pondered how Stuart De La Deccio was taking it. The head of the largest eyewear conglomerate in the world must be panicking right about now. His factories supplied the bulk of the world's prescription eyewear.

Dalton stared impatiently at the elevator numbers, wondering how much longer it might be. *It was going to be a bright, clear, beautiful day,* he thought as he patted his jacket pocket to make sure he had grabbed his sunglasses. *Well, at least De La Deccio would still have his sunglasses division*, Dalton said to himself as the elevator doors opened.

Dalton stepped into the plush lobby of SoJo Technology's headquarters. It radiated opulence mixed with the cutting-edge crispness of state-of-the-art technology. *This place never failed to impress*, he reflected as he stepped up to the receptionist. He glanced at the receptionist's nameplate and warmly greeted him: "Good morning, Steven! How are you today? I am here to see Kelli Jackson." Steven smiled. "I'm doing well. Your name?"

After completing the security protocol, Steven directed Dalton to the door to Kelli's office. Kelli was deeply engrossed in the content displayed on her 40-inch curved monitor. *That's an impressive swoopy screen,* Dalton thought. The darn thing dominated more than half of her desk.

It was always good to see Kelli. "Kelli! I saw SoJo's recent media release. Congrats! Your product is going to revolutionize the industry!" Kelli stood and gave Dalton a warm embrace. "Thanks, D. So glad you could make the trip up. The PR is the lone bright spot on a roller-coaster period for us. Try as I might, I cannot fathom that the accusations against Julianne are true. She's been with this firm since the beginning."

Dalton sat down and adjusted the sharp crease of his black pinstripe suit pants. He signed and nodded his head. Leaning forward, he said, "We've known each other forever. Tell me what's going on. I know we briefly covered the key details on our call on Friday. Now let's fill in the blanks so I can understand your suspicions in greater depth."

Kelli pulled up her chair, uncrossed her legs, and leaned on her desk to assemble her thoughts. She rested her folded hands on the desk and began:

"As you know, our annual employee survey results came back this past October. Every year we get the standard complaints about this and that. This year, we received very specific information that necessitated a deeper look into the sales department. While our survey is anonymous, we are able to easily determine which division they pertain to. Two team members indicated departmental ethics of the accused are less than stellar. Their comments were very specific. They accused Julianne Cranson of encouraging kickbacks, providing undocumented discounts to customers, submitting fraudulent travel expense reports, and possibly most disturbing of all, threatening and intimidating her team members.

Dalton, looking a bit perplexed, asked, "Why do you think they chose the survey and not the ethics hotline?" Kelli shook her head, rolled her eyes, and said, "This is on the back burner, but we are definitely planning on looking into this. If employees do not call the hotline for these types of issues, we have to question the effectiveness of our hotline." Dalton took this as something to follow up on after the current issue was resolved.

Kelli leaned back and quickly entered a few keystrokes to pull up her notes. Glancing away from the screen, she continued: "We take employee comments on the survey very seriously. The specificity of the accusations highlighted by

Julianne's team members is more than a little disturbing. My first thought was that the two were conspiring, perhaps setting up Julianne or one of her directs, in an effort to topple a good executive. It's not unheard of to orchestrate such a move to open a position in the executive ranks. But a deeper dive by our IT team discovered that the survey results, as indicated by the associated geolocator codes embedded in the survey acknowledgment, were from two team members in completely different offices. This lowers the likelihood of collusion."

Dalton pondered this information for a few moments. Kelli continued, "We don't have a formal fraud department, so Edward pulled the sales results from Julianne's team. You know Edward, don't you? He's our chief operating officer. He joined us a few years back from Optical Solutions." "Of course," Dalton replied, "I believe I ran into him at an industry event just a few months ago. Great guy. His son plays soccer for Freedom Force. They won the cup this year."

Kelli chuckled. Dalton remembered little details about everyone. It was uncanny at times. "Yes, his son is on track to receive several college scholarship offers. At any rate, Edward and I reviewed the sales reports. Julianne always has positive growth and exceptional performance. Over the past few years, the increases have not been large, but she is still the best at SoJo and is known as one of the best in the industry. This year is no different. Her numbers show a steady increase. She is on track to receive her full sales bonus, plus go on the annual company sales incentive trip. However, due to the survey accusations, I asked our controller to review Julianne's expense reports. Everything looked normal at first glance. But yesterday Christine found a few unusual entries. Four hotel expenses reported this quarter matched a hotel folio from January. Christine said she wouldn't have noticed, but a smudge from smeared printer ink caught her eye. It seems that smudge also appeared on another receipt. After going back and reevaluating all of Julianne's expenses, Christine identified multiple entries supported by the same receipt. The dates had been altered, but the details remained the same."

Dalton thought that discrepancy should have been caught—same expense amount multiple times? Dalton then recalled the many previous conversations he had with Kelli. One of her main objectives was to build the infrastructure to support a company whose sales had outgrown its surroundings. SoJo still used a rudimentary accounting software and had minimal data analytics options other than manually created spreadsheets. He rested his elbow on his knee. His hand gently brushed his goatee as he considered this information.

Kelli interrupted his thoughts. "Over the weekend, Christine did a deeper dive. She pulled expense reports from the last two years and identified nearly

$72,000 in questionable expenses. We give our sales team a ton of leeway in order to get the job done, so we do not ask a lot of questions, but it's also clear from our management team that everything has to stay above board. Our reputation is too valuable to risk, especially in this period of significant growth and innovation."

Kelli went on with her narrative. "Given that Christine seemed to have substantiated one of the claims from the employee survey, I asked Edward to look into Julianne's customer relationships. We have a standard pricing practice. Deviations from the sales price cards require documentation and approval. However, since Julianne is an Executive Vice President (EVP), she is not required to obtain additional approvals for exception pricing she personally recommends. Edward noted that a couple of key accounts received unusual discounts. I want to caution you not to read too much into this; it is normal for the sales team to have discretion over pricing. However, it does go against company practices because the discounts do not seem to be supported with comments or explanations indicating why a discount was warranted. The discounts are excessive based on our history and are not in line with anything else the sales team has offered over the past five years. By itself, this would be just a minor note and a quick conversation with Julianne. However, combined with the survey results and the expense reporting anomalies, we feel a full investigation may be warranted."

Dalton steepled his hands and looked Kelli in the eyes. "I agree. Has HR looked into the employee practices allegation? If not, I'd prefer they refrain so Julianne isn't tipped off that something is amiss." Kelli picked up her pen and jotted a quick note. Dalton continued, "Can I get copies of the documents both Christine and Edward reviewed? Did they formalize their conclusions in a report?" Kelli stopped and stared at him. "No, I'm sorry. They both sent me emails requesting calendar time to cover the details and their conclusions in face-to-face meetings."

"Perfect. I can appreciate not wanting to put something like that in an email." Dalton took the paper copies Kelli handed him of the expense reports, sales reports, and customer records. He looked at the pages briefly. "Do you by chance also have the survey?"

"Of course," Kelli replied. She began typing. Reaching over to the printer, she grabbed the survey and passed it to Dalton. "What else do you need?"

Dalton thought about what else might be required and his next steps. As an executive coach and trainer, he no longer dealt with this type of situation on a day-to-day basis. He did have plenty of experience in investigative techniques because he worked on the fraud investigations team in a few of his previous roles and now played the role of expert witness in many prosecutions. He was excited about this challenge and the other opportunities he and Kelli had discussed the previous week.

"Who knows about this? It's important that Julianne remains unaware of the situation until we interview her." Kelli's hands toyed with her wedding ring, spinning it around and around her finger. This was a common sign of nervousness. Since their relationship went back many years, he knew Kelli commonly played with her jewelry when under stress.

"Given the focus on our recent product development efforts, we have not had a chance to discuss this with the full executive team. As of right now, only Simon, Edward, Christine, and Joseph, our legal officer, are aware of the situation."

Dalton nodded and then asked, "Simon is the HR EVP, correct?" Kelli nodded. "Okay, let's keep the audience small. You'll need to ask each of them to refrain from sharing the information with anyone else."

Kelli sighed. "Dalton, we cannot afford for this to leak to the media. I'll pull everyone together this morning to emphasize the gravity of the situation."

Dalton's eyes reflected complete understanding. He softened his features and leaned forward. "Kelli, we will do everything we can to protect your company. You did the right thing by contacting me to do the fraud investigation. Many companies try to keep everything in-house, but then find that they need professional assistance when the magnitude of the fraud is uncovered. If your suspicions are confirmed, do you plan to prosecute?"

Kelli looked surprised. "Why would I prosecute? We need to keep this out of the press."

"I suspected that is what you would say. If Julianne has committed these acts and you do not prosecute, then she will likely repeat these practices against her next employer."

Kelli nodded. "I appreciate the feedback. I'll need to bring Brandon up to speed. As CEO, the decision is his to make."

"Please tell Brandon to reach out to me if he would like to discuss his options. There are too many unknowns to decide now, but the tide is turning on crisis management. I realize you don't want this to get out, but is it better to contain the message or, depending on what the message is, get ahead of it and make sure it is the right message?"

Kelli leaned her head slightly to the right and furrowed her brow. She responded only through her body language, not with words. Dalton gave her a winning smile, the smile that brought confidence to his face and to the minds of his clients. He liked to call it his "Blue Steel," a reference to some movie he could not remember the name of.

"For now, let's walk through our next steps," Dalton continued. "At a very high level, our investigation will follow a standard process:

- Planning
- Obtaining and analyzing evidence
  - Data analytics/electronic forensic discovery
  - Interviews
- Reporting

"We will approach this from two opposite directions. We will assume that the fraud has occurred and has not occurred. Our goal is to obtain evidence supporting our hypotheses. You see, both sides of fraud must be examined. By law, proof of fraud must preclude any explanation other than guilt.

"We will spend the next couple days planning our approach and reviewing the results of Edward's and Christine's analyses. We'd also like to look at the raw data to do further data analytics. This assessment will include an evaluation to address the potential kickbacks that were cited in the employee survey results. If you could arrange for a data dump of the sales records, vendor records, and expense reports going back five years, that would be ideal. We will review the data for suspicious records, unusual transactions, trends, anything that could look suspicious and can confirm or deny our hypotheses.

"Once we have the results, I'd like to interview Julianne as well as a few of her employees. Our discussion with Julianne will be followed by having her give a written statement. We will record the interview just in case Brandon opts to prosecute. As a matter of fact, we will prepare our entire investigation with the assumption that your firm could pursue prosecution."

Dalton and Kelli discussed some of the other opportunities she wanted his assistance on. Dalton assured Kelli that abnormal is the norm in today's corporate America. "These things happen. Just like I told Caleb after he had a subpar game a few weeks back, everyone makes mistakes. How you react to those mistakes is what truly matters." They discussed some potential coaching opportunities and presentation and speaking training she wanted to do for her senior leadership team's continued development. He spent some time with her senior team and headed off, excited to have his team dive headfirst into the data.

A week later, Dalton returned to SoJo. He met Simon, the head of SoJo's HR department, on the third floor. "Julianne has received a meeting invitation to interview a prospective candidate. We followed your instructions and set the meeting in a private conference room. She should be arriving in the next few minutes." Simon showed him into the room and sat quietly with Dalton. Simon needed to attend the meeting to have someone from Human Resources involved so Julianne could not claim harassment or duress.

Dalton got up and took a look around the room, then pulled a chair to the end of the table. *I don't want her hiding her hands under the table while we talk*, he thought. *I need to see any telltale signs of deception, so her hands and feet need to be visible.* He had specifically requested a conference room that would give him the space to sit facing the door but farthest away from it, and strategically place another chair kitty-corner from him at the table. Once the room was set to his liking, he sat near the empty chair and faced the door. While he waited, he once again reviewed the data analysis of Julianne's expense reporting. His team's analytics identified nearly a hundred questionable transactions. Julianne had a habit of reusing receipts for expense reporting. Her People-Centric skills were fairly good, but she sometimes neglected to pay attention to the details. Her cover-up abilities seemed to get worse with time. This was a telltale sign of a person who had gotten away with everything for a long time and was getting a bit too comfortable with their deception. Her abnormal behavior was being normalized.

Based on his team's work, it looked like Julianne had a haphazard approach to modifying hotel receipts, often forgetting to change the folio numbers or using earlier sequenced numbers. Why on earth would an accounting system count backwards? Dalton shook his head, wondering how Julianne could miss something so basic. His team uncovered several other anomalies, including records supporting unusual discounts and large refunds to customers. He made a note and adjusted the list of questions he planned to use to get Julianne's thoughts on these transactions.

Julianne stepped into the room and said, "Hello. My name is Julianne Cranson. How are you today?" Dalton stood and took her hand. Julianne was very professional, with light blondish-red hair and dressed in a brown pant suit.

"It is a pleasure to meet you. My name is Dalton Zimmer."

Julianne firmly grasped his hand and was grateful he returned the firm handshake. Too often men assumed that they should gently clasp a woman's hand. Frankly, limp handshakes gave her the creeps and felt somewhat offensive. She then noticed Simon was in the room and thought how odd it was to see him here. "It is a pleasure to meet you, Mr. Zimmer!" Julianne's bubbly personality radiated throughout the room. Simon got up and closed the door and then took his seat at the opposite end of the table.

Julianne looked confused. The mood in the room was about to change. Dalton took a moment to study her and said, "Unfortunately, I'm not here today to interview for a position in your firm. Please have a seat Mrs. Cranson."

Kelli walked briskly to meet with the team and discuss Dalton's conversation with Julianne. She was nervous with heightened anticipation. Shortly after, Joseph, Edward, and Brandon filed in and waited for Dalton to arrive. The air was thick with tension. Uncomfortable with the silence, Simon stated *Julianne took it well when we placed her on leave of absence.*

Brandon sighed and tossed his pen onto the conference room table. The unexpected clatter startled everyone, including Kelli. Brandon looked at Simon, saying, "I still can't believe it. She is a great employee and she is the main reason our market share consistently beats the competition. Dalton had better have hard evidence that supports this situation because I am not happy at all."

At 9:01 am Dalton stepped into the room. "Good morning. How is everyone?" Dalton felt the tension but was used to it and it did not ruffle his professional demeanor. He was chipper but serious. He viewed situations like these as a puzzle and he liked enjoyed complication.

Brandon glared at Dalton. Simon gently spoke up. "Good morning Dalton. Thank you for joining us. Do you have information that will resolve this situation?" Dalton laid his computer bag on the floor and pulled out his laptop. He took a deep breath and began. "I know this is a difficult situation and you are anxious for our results, so I won't keep you waiting any longer. My goal is to present you with the facts on what has occurred, and how Julianne reacted, and then we can talk about next steps." He connected his Mac to the projector screen and opened the file to his report.

Brandon leaned back in his chair and crossed his arms and legs. Dalton noted he looked less than pleased. Glancing around the room, he observed that the body language from everyone was closed off and somewhat defensive. *Well,* he thought, *this will be fun.*

"Let me start by walking you through the investigative work we completed. As you know, we agreed our scope would include the following:

- Data mining and data analysis using the data dumps you provided us at the onset of our engagement

- Interviews with key individuals, including Julianne. We obtained Julianne's consent and videoed these sessions for your records.
- Written statements from key individuals, including Julianne

"Let's start with the data. We requested five years of transaction records covering sales, vendor payments, and expense reports. We found more than a hundred suspicious transactions.

- Our review identified what appears to be modified hotel receipts used to support 34 different business trips expensed over the last 36 months. My team validated that a handful of the hotel's folio numbers were left unchanged. However, 28 of them showed folio sequence numbers that don't align with the timing of the transaction. You see, hotel folios are invoices and are assigned numerically. Hence, as time goes by, the folio number should increase. But the hotel receipts associated with Julianne's expense reports reflect folio numbers that are nonsequential and do not seem to correlate to her business trip dates.
- We also identified unusual refunds and sizable discounts issued to three of your largest customers. We reviewed your sales records, invoices, customer refunds, and inventory levels looking for any unusual patterns. We pinpointed three customers who, considering their sales volume and history, seem to have been issued higher-than-normal refunds in relation to the remaining customer population. All three of these customers belong to Julianne. Specifically, she is the primary contact managing these relationships. The customers in question are:
  - Seibert Industries: 28 refunds
  - Lushane Optical: 8 refunds
  - Curtis Laboratories: 6 refunds

  What we found most interesting about these refunds is that none of the 42 transactions resulted in a change in your inventory levels. In each case, the refund was processed, with Julianne's approval, and the billing adjusted, but the sales returns account didn't change and neither did the physical inventory level.

  We also noted that all three of these customers received special pricing on 46 invoices over the last three years. Our analysis identified 17 invoices for Seibert, 13 for Lushane, and 16 for Curtis, with discounts falling outside of SoJo company policy. In some cases, these discounts resulted in SoJo selling inventory below cost. We reviewed the discount approvals and in each case the reduction was authorized by either Julianne or by one of her directs. That being said, company policy requires discounts be explained and justified. The notes for all of the transactions in question merely state, "Discounted per Julianne Cranson."

Brandon interrupted Dalton. Dalton saw this coming, as Brandon's body language indicated his displeasure: he was continually rolling his eyes. "This does not seem like anything that would result in prosecuting for fraud. Your analysis is interesting, but I suspect there is a reasonable explanation for these transactions. It is well within Julianne's job duties to authorize customer discounts. These hardly indicate that Julianne has committed fraud."

Dalton slowly turned and pondered Brandon's comments. "I understand your position and I am not saying she committed fraud. That is for the court to decide, should you opt to prosecute. However, these transactions do seem a bit odd, don't you think?" Brandon leaned back in his chair, steepling his fingers and resting his chin against his index fingers. "Mr. Zimmer, I agree that these look unusual, and I am interested in hearing what Julianne had to say about them. I will reserve my judgment for now. Please continue."

"Of course. Let's watch the video to see my interview with Julianne on the 2nd of this month. Pay close attention to Julianne's facial expressions—they provide a key to determining whether she is being truthful or deceptive. Using the BASIC method, I will show you how I combined facial recognition with advanced interrogation techniques to identify areas where Julianne was deceptive during our interview.

"The video starts out with Julianne walking into the room. Watch her facial features as I explain that I am not here to interview for a company position. She first expresses surprise. You will see her eyebrows go up, her eyes open, and her lips part as she sits down. When she notices Simon in the room, you will see a fleeting glimpse of what could be a sign of fear cross Julianne's features. She is likely wondering why Simon is participating in the meeting, why she was really called in, and why there is a camera in the room." Dalton pointed to the screen as the video continued to play. "Now watch as her eyes seem to change emotion. Her upper eyelids open to expose more of her eyes and her lips stretch horizontally while she pulls her chin and head back. The movement is subtle and very brief. It is possible she believes her situation has been exposed. However, given the short duration of the emotion, it is also possible she's rationalizing her surprise over the meeting's turn of events.

"Before my questioning begins, she seems to have moved into curiosity mode. She appears confident and seems to have banished any thought that her suspicious activities have been detected. Look how her facial stance moves into relaxed confidence and her features are symmetrical." He paused the video and turned to the group. "Research performed by Paul Ekman isolated nine facial indicators providing reliable clues to decision:

- **Micro-expressions:** Involuntary expressions that briefly flash across the subject's face.
- **Squelched expressions:** Indicates that a person is trying to hide his or her emotions, but in contrast to a micro-expression, a squelched expression is performed on purpose and involves the signaling of multiple emotions.
- **Reliable muscle patterns:** Reliable muscles are not easy to control. These include the muscle that narrows the eyelids, the orbicularis oculi, and produces crow's feet at the outer corners of the eye. The orbicularis oculi is difficult to move into a smile deliberately when your emotional state does not support smiling. The entire face must be watched carefully for clues of deception. When someone is attempting to deceive, their true emotions and thoughts are often displayed via the reliable muscle patterns on the upper portion of the face (forehead, eyebrows, eyes).
- **Blink rates:** Blinking can be voluntary or involuntary, but deception can trigger higher rates of blinking.
- **Pupil dilation:** Pupil dilation is a reliable indicator. We are not aware of anyone who can control the size of their pupils. Unusually dilated pupils are generally associated with fear but can also be caused by other uncontrolled emotions.
- **Tears:** While tears are obvious indicators of distress, they are not hard to fake. Take note of tears, but do not be misled by them.
- **Asymmetrical expressions:** Genuine emotion, apart from contempt, is displayed by both sides of the face. Attempts to conceal emotion or portray a particular emotion is often limited to one side of a person's face.
- **Timing:** True emotion is expressed simultaneously. The timing difference for feigned emotion is brief, but it is there if you watch for it.
- **Duration:** Genuine emotion generally lasts between five and ten seconds. A fixed expression held beyond ten seconds may indicate that the subject is attempting to hide their true thoughts and feelings."[1]

Dalton scanned the group to gauge their understanding before continuing. "Caution must be observed with any and all of these indicators. Detecting

---

[1] Adapted from Meyer, P. (2010). *Liespotting: Proven Techniques for Detecting Deception.* (New York: St. Martin's Press)

deception requires an understanding of the person's baseline behavior when being truthful. As you observed, I started our conversation by asking Julianne a series of questions designed to elicit truthful responses. This allows me to baseline her facial features and body language.

"Body language is also important. We must watch for clusters of behavior that indicate deception. Your body reveals your inner thoughts. Behavior or gestures inconsistent with spoken words is a tip that the subject may be lying. It is estimated that a significant percentage of communication is nonverbal and is mostly conveyed through body language." Dalton was standing and presenting and he leaned forward, putting his hands on the back of the chair in front of him. "One last thing to note about body language. A person's gestures and body movement naturally emphasize their spoken words. When a person's hands and body do not align with the words they use, deception is suspected."

Dalton stood and walked to the front of the room as he juggled the remote control. "Conversely, stillness of the body and hands is also concerning. A lack of movement often indicates that the brain is trying to control the body's responses. At times, this control is successful for half of the body, such as a one-sided shoulder shrug, or a single hand movement when both hands are normally used.

"Aside from observing Julianne's facial features and body language, I encourage you to listen closely and resist the urge to fill in missing information when hearing her responses. Pay attention to *exactly* what is said and, more important, what is not said."

Dalton restarted the video and turned up the volume. Julianne could be seen stepping into the room. The camera perfectly captured her facial expressions as she introduced herself. Friendly emotions show before confusion and, just as Dalton said, a momentary glimpse of uncertainty or fear briefly flickered before she sat down, and her countenance began to exude confidence mixed with a heavy dose of curiosity.

Dalton talked as the video played. "As I mentioned earlier, my initial questions are designed to baseline her body language and facial expressions. As I explained to Kelli the last time we met, the BASIC method of interrogation differs significantly from other types of interviews, such as those conducted during an internal audit. In an audit interview, the person you are questioning is considered an expert and is treated as such. The interview is structured as a conversation designed to get the person to relax, to allow the auditor to obtain as much information as possible about the topic at hand. Process-flow conversations or discussions about journal entries focus on how transactions flow or why they are booked, to enable an auditor to gain an understanding of the process, journal entry, and so on. Emotion should not play an integral role in these types of interviews."

Dalton looked around the room and determined that a more in-depth explanation was needed before proceeding. *The last thing I need,* he thought, *is for these folks to confuse a fraud investigation technique with normal business practices.* He paused the video and picked up a marker before walking over to the white board. Drawing out a table he stated, "Let me show you what I mean."

Internal Audit Interview	Fraud Investigation Interview
Objective: To gain an understanding	Objective: To obtain information regarding involvement or noninvolvement
Friendly, conversational format	Friendly and conversational format to baseline and establish rapport
Designed to obtain information and build/retain the client relationship	Open-ended questions used to obtain/assess facts
Tone and wording crafted to get audit client to relax	Yes/No questions used to assess behavior
Questions focus on gaining an understanding of a process, journal entry, or accounting rationale	**BASIC framework/methodology**
Open-ended questions used to collect facts	▪ **B**aseline behavior (laughter, movement, tone, pitch, reaction times, expressions)
	▪ **A**sk open-ended questions
	▪ **S**tudy the clusters
	▪ **I**ntuit the gaps: if something doesn't add up, ask more questions
	▪ **C**onfirm[2]

Confident in his explanations, Dalton restarted the video from the beginning and then fast-forwarded until Julianne was seen sitting down. He hit play just as he was heard saying, "Julianne, let me start by explaining who I am and why I am here. I've been hired by your company to gain an understanding of your sales process and to look for opportunities for internal control weaknesses. Do you mind if we record our conversation?" Julianne shook her head no. Dalton prompted her. "Would you mind speaking your response? We prefer to obtain oral consent to record."

Julianne replied, "No, I do not mind."

"Thank you." Dalton looked toward the other end of the table and said, "Simon is here just to observe. So let's get started. Can you tell me a little about yourself? How long have you been with SoJo?"

---

[2] Ibid.

Julianne took a breath and went over her resume and background. Her body language was relaxed as Dalton established rapport. The video showed them laughing and talking as if they had been friends for ages. As the interview progressed, Dalton opened his folder. "Julianne, the company has reviewed their sales transactions and I wondered if you might help me with a few of them?" Julianne's face lit up. "Of course, Dalton. I am happy to help. Let me take a look." Dalton removed a printed invoice for Seibert Industries from his folder. He slid the paper over to Julianne. She leaned over the document and looked up. "Julianne, can you tell me about this sale to Seibert Industries?" Julianne leaned back and moved her chair, slightly angling it toward the door. She twisted her torso to rest her waist against the conference room table. Dalton stopped the video.

"As you can see, Julianne has modified her previously open body language to a closed off position. Her feet are pointed toward the door and she has firmly placed the conference room table in between us. Her upper body faces me, but her lower body desires to escape the room." Dalton hit play as Julianne explained that Seibert is her top customer. "They buy corrective eyewear supplies. This invoice is for $3.5 million in frames." Dalton took the invoice she handed back to him. He reviewed it momentarily and then pointed to the discount. "What do you think about the discount shown here?"

Julianne glanced at the numbers. "It seems reasonable. Seibert is a top customer and they buy more than $100 million in product from me every year."

Dalton nodded his head. "I see you approved the discount?"

"Yes," she replied. "Again, it is normal and customary for Seibert to receive discounts."

Dalton pulled the company policy document out of his folder. "Julianne, I hear what you are saying, but I wondered if you could help me with something. Your company policy says that discounts must be fully documented with justification supporting the discount included in the account notes. Can you take a look at the account notes for me?"

Julianne took the second paper and read the notes. "It looks fine. I approved the discount."

Dalton smiled. "Yes, I believe you did. Can you show me the justification supporting the discount?"

Julianne looked annoyed. "As far as I'm concerned the discount is justified. I am an EVP and well within my authority to approve a discount."

Dalton removed a second invoice from his folder. "Julianne, what can you tell me about Lushane Optical?"

Julianne reviewed the invoice and looked up sharply at Dalton. "Lushane Optical purchases about $64 million in product from me each year. I authorized a discount for certain frames and lenses."

Dalton watched her reaction. She was beginning to perspire. Gone was the friendly tone and the rapport they had experienced earlier.

Julianne continued, "I really do have to go. I apologize but I have another meeting to attend." She rose and headed for the door.

Simon spoke gently as she reached for the door handle. "Julianne, I believe Edward took care of your morning meetings. Please have a seat so Mr. Zimmer can finish his questions."

Julianne slowly returned to her chair. Dalton handed her a third invoice. "This one shows discounts for Curtis Laboratories. Can you tell me about them?"

Julianne grabbed the paper and tossed it onto the table. "It is the same situation. They are a large customer. I authorized discounts for their products."

Dalton calmly picked the paper up and returned it to the folder. "All told, it seems you authorized discounts for these vendors that exceeded 30% and you sold your company's products below cost. What is the business case supporting these deep discounts?"

Julianne replied, "You know, if you think about it, I am the wrong person to ask. You should speak with Edward. He is aware of the importance of these clients."

Dalton wrote a brief note on his pad. He smiled. "Thank you. I appreciate your assistance. I'll ask Edward."

Dalton changed topics. "I wondered if you could also help me understand a few of the refunds these customers received. Here is one for Curtis Laboratories. They received an invoice adjustment of $25,000 for what is noted as defective frames. What do you know about this transaction?"

Julianne once again took the paper, reviewed it, and put it down in front of her. She looked at Dalton and smiled. "Mr. Zimmer, I am sure you are aware that we are not perfect. SoJo has its fair share of defective merchandise."

Dalton studied her features as he said, "Yes, yes. I am sure you do, Julianne. However, I find it odd that the merchandise was not actually returned to SoJo." Dalton watched her eyes closely. "We seem to have the same situation with both Seibert Industries and Lushane Optical. As a matter of fact, these three companies represented more than 87% of the total returns for SoJo this fiscal year. I was wondering if you could help me understand how these three companies could receive such a large portion of your company's defective merchandise?"

Julianne retorted, "Again, I am not in charge of operations. I am a sales representative. I sell the product. As a matter of fact, I am thrilled you are looking into this because it has been a rather large problem for myself and my team. Imagine having to face my largest clients and accept responsibility for the faulty workmanship produced by the operations team. I've had numerous conversations with the head of production, but his quality control measures continue to fail. I recommend speaking to him about the problems in his shop."

Dalton stopped the video. He turned to the executives. "As you can see, Julianne is quite angry and defensive. She hasn't answered any of my questions."

"Now wait a minute, Zimmer," Brandon said. "Of course she is angry and defensive. She is in charge of sales. She does not manage the production line."

Edward interrupted. "Brandon, there isn't a problem on the production line. None of the other clients have complained about the quality. I've reviewed the numbers. I personally walked the production line, and internal audit reviewed the quality control procedures."

Brandon wiped his face with his hands and then pulled his fingers through what was left of his hair. "This whole thing makes no sense. Why would Julianne do this? She makes plenty of money."

"If I may," Dalton said, "I would like to continue. This next section of the interview focuses on her expense reporting." He turned the video back on. Julianne was now sitting squarely facing the door. Her arms were crossed and her face clearly showed her displeasure. Her shoulders were nearly perpendicular to Dalton. On the video, Dalton was now reaching into his folder and pulling out several hotel invoices. "Julianne, do you recognize these receipts?"

Julianne's angry eyes immediately flashed. "Of course I do. That is a hotel receipt from my favorite hotel in Manhattan."

Dalton laid six of the hotel receipts side by side. "And," he asked, "do you recognize these?" Julianne's scowl remained firmly in place, but her eyes changed; a slight flicker was evident in her eye muscle. She blinked several times and said, mimicking Dalton's question, "Do I recognize these? Hmm. They look like the receipt we just talked about for the St. Regis hotel in Manhattan." Julianne uncrossed her arms and folded her hands into her lap.

Dalton stopped the video and explained, "Up to this point I think you will agree that Julianne has been evasive. She's refused to directly answer any of my questions. Her oral responses included several verbal cues that indicate she is working hard at denying accountability. At this point, I am confident she knows she has a problem. Watch her body language as we begin to talk further about her expense reports."

The video resumed and Julianne could be seen assuming an almost royal stance with her back straight, mouth planted in a firm scowl, hands gently folded in her lap, and ankles crossed.

Dalton continued, "Yes. They do look like the same receipt, right down to the folio number. Only, the dates seem to be different. And right here, there is an ink smudge. How do you think that smudge happened to be on six different receipts spanning more than 24 months?"

Julianne didn't move. She stared him down for several seconds before replying. "You will need to ask the hotel. I am not familiar with their front desk practices."

Dalton then pulled the remaining 28 hotel receipts from his folder. "Julianne, I have 28 more hotel receipts here. They also span the last 24 months and they seem to have a few unusual things in common. They are largely identical, with the exception of the folio numbers. But the thing I don't understand is why the folio numbers seem to be out of sequence. Let me show you. Here we have a receipt from July 24. The folio number is 009-9898. Next we have a receipt from the same hotel dated August 11 but the folio number is 002-0099, and one dated October 10 with a folio number of 009-9891. What do you think might have caused this?" Dalton's tone was very even, stating facts without attempting to lead Julianne or sound condescending.

Julianne stared for a long time at the invoices. She coldly looked up at Dalton and said, "It must be a sad, sad life you lead. Do you spend all your days harassing executives about their expense reports? I don't spend my time reviewing hotel receipts. I travel frequently to New York, Mr. Zimmer. I stay at the Regis because it is close to Seibert Industries and I am required to entertain my clients at nearby restaurants. The Regis is convenient and comfortable—"

Dalton stopped her. "How often do you travel to New York?"

"I think you already know the answer to that question. Clearly you have been through my expense reports with a fine-tooth comb."[3]

Dalton closed the folder. The video showed him quietly looking at Julianne. Her body language and facial expressions revealed indignation, but it only reached the lower half of her face. Julianne's mouth was slightly open and her lower jaw was tense, but her eyes remained shrewdly focused and failed to show the normal wide-eyed stance often displayed when someone feels they've

---

[3] McClish, M. (2001). *I Know You Are Lying*. (Harrisburg, NC: Marpa Group, Inc.).

been falsely accused. "Julianne, we can stop this right now if you will be honest and upfront with me. How is it that 34 expense reports are supported by the same two hotel receipts?"

"I do not know. My admin prepares my expense reports. Perhaps she lost my receipts and covered her tracks using a duplicate copy? How should I know?"

Dalton tilted his head sideways, showing interest. "You believe your administrative assistant forged receipts for your expense reports?" Julianne's eyes relaxed as she said, "Of course! That is exactly what happened. She handles everything like that for me." Dalton nodded. "I see. I am sure you would be interested to know that I took your administrative assistant's written statement earlier this week. Would you like to see it?"

Julianne's face fell. "Yes," she quietly replied. "Yes, I would like to see it." Dalton thumbed through his folder and pulled out a handwritten paper. "Do you recognize Megan Zamora's handwriting?" Julianne held the paper for a long time. She read the statement. "Julianne, can you read the last paragraph out loud for me?" Dalton said. Julianne began reading Megan's statement, which explained that Julianne insisted on completing her own expense reports. The paragraph recounted how Megan once attempted to help Julianne out with her travel expenses. Megan indicated that Julianne flew into a rage so fierce that she threw her crystal paperweight across the room, nearly hitting Megan's shoulder as it shattered against the wall behind her. Megan ended the paragraph with a brief statement saying she didn't believe Julianne meant to throw it at her, but as a result of the incident, she never offered to help with Julianne's expenses again.

Dalton took a pad of paper and a pen and slid them across the table to Julianne. "Julianne, I'd like you to write down your thoughts on how 34 expense reports are supported by the same two receipts. I'd also like you to explain the customer discounts and the returns for your three largest clients."

Dalton turned off the video. "At this point, I've asked Julianne to write her own statement explaining how these things might have occurred. Once she was done, Simon and I left her alone in the room while my associate and I reviewed the written statement. Our analysis identified several inconsistencies in Julianne's written statement, which we later discussed with her.

"I'd like to go over a couple of key highlights from her statement." Dalton pulled up his electronic report on the display. Pointing to the screen, he said, "When asked if her submitted falsified receipts for her hotel expenses at the St. Regis in New York City, Julianne's written statement indicated:

Apparently, there is a system glitch or something that caused the same receipts to be attached to my expense reports. I am trying to be as honest as possible. We are fortunate that you identified the situation and we can now take measures to rectify it. We've relied on external guidance almost from the start and from the moment Edward suggested that it would be foolish to do things in-house, I thought we shouldn't rely on outside firms.

"In her written response, Julianne is casting blame for her expense report receipts on a system glitch or an unnamed third party but qualifies it with the word 'apparently,' indicating that she is just speculating. However, what comes next is most interesting. Julianne states, 'I am trying to be as honest as possible.' What Julianne just told us is that her first sentence was not as honest as it could or should be. The word 'trying' means attempted but not completed. People say what they mean to say. Julianne used the word 'trying' to give the appearance that she was being truthful.

"In my follow-up conversation with her, I asked, 'Julianne, have you ever falsified a receipt for your expense report?' Her response was, 'I don't believe I have ever intentionally submitted falsified receipts.'

"In this example, Julianne again failed to answer my question. She is using plausible deniability to answer the question honestly but leaving an out. She is going to focus her comments on an error or that she honestly lost track of the expense reports and did not do this on purpose." Dalton wanted to make sure the senior management team understood the importance of plausible deniability and of what they had just heard. Julianne was answering the question honestly, but she gave herself an out. SoJo could not come back and say she was lying unless they were able to prove she did this intentionally, which can be challenging. It was key to listen for other answers to yes/no questions, because people answer questions in very specific ways.

Julianne's written statement addressed the customer discounts. She wrote:

Customers can purchase products from multiple suppliers, so they sometimes need pricing incentives to close the sale. Supplier discounts received for raw materials are available to offset these end sale incentives, allowing the company to make a narrow profit while retaining the customer relationship. My team does not provide discounts when they are not warranted. Sales are a key component of this firm's profitability and we work hard to ensure sales growth continues.

Dalton went on. "Notice here that Julianne says, 'My team does not provide discounts when they are not warranted.' This is a classic avoidance technique to give the appearance of answering the question while allowing her to avoid admitting personal guilt. Julianne says her team does not provide unwarranted discounts without addressing the fact that she admitted during our earlier recorded conversation that she authorized these deep discounts without explaining why they were warranted.

"I asked her the following question to clarify her statement: 'Julianne, was the 30% discount to Seibert Industries justified?' She responded, 'I intend to fully explain why I approved the discount for Seibert Industries. As I have indicated previously, Seibert Industries is a valuable customer and SoJo must retain the relationship. Sometimes discounts are needed to obtain the sale.' In this statement, Julianne said 'I intend' to fully explain. She may have great intentions but using the word 'intend' does not mean that she is going to carry out the task.

"We next turn to Julianne's written statement regarding customer refunds. These refunds could be construed as customer kickbacks, as alleged in the employee survey."

> SoJo has a great reputation in the industry. It is sometimes necessary to process refunds for products with manufacturing defects. I am not familiar with what goes on in Operations and cannot explain why Seibert Industries, Lushane Optical, and Curtis Laboratories comprise the bulk of SoJo's returns.

"Julianne clearly states, 'I cannot explain why,' indicating that she is perhaps being deceptive.

"In my follow-up questioning, I asked her, 'Did you authorize kickbacks in the form of customer refunds to Curtis Laboratories?'

"Julianne's indignant response revealed her true feelings: 'I really don't have to take this. What do you take me for? Do you honestly think that I am going to answer your question? Only a fool would give customers kickbacks.'

"Julianne's delaying tactics and ultimate response, 'Only a fool would give customers kickbacks,' highlights her inability to be truthful. The response should have been a simple yes or no. However, Julianne avoids telling the truth by not responding to the question. She is now being defiant."

Dalton paused. He closed his laptop and turned off the projector. "Brandon, according to Donald Cressy and the Association of Certified Fraud Examiners, the fraud triangle model can be used to explain the factors that cause someone to commit occupational fraud. It consists of three components which, together, lead to fraudulent behavior:

1. Perceived unsharable financial need
2. Perceived opportunity
3. Rationalization [4]

"When I evaluated this case, I went back to my initial conversations with Kelli. As you will recall, Julianne's husband filed for divorce three years ago. The messy case is still tied up in the courts. She has an $8 million-dollar estate in one of the wealthiest neighborhoods in the city. As the breadwinner for the family, she shared her frustration that it is her responsibility to pay the mortgage and provide for her four children's private school tuition. The family travels extensively and, in the past, her husband and children spent their summers at their estate in Japan. In my opinion, this financial pressure could be perceived by Julianne as an unsharable financial need. I know her husband is very successful, but it seems like the divorce caused significant financial strain.

"As for opportunity, Julianne's position allowed her to potentially falsify expense reports, as well as authorize discounts and approve customer returns, both of which could be construed as alleged kickbacks. Her position enabled her to effectively circumvent your firm's policies and procedures. In addition, statements gathered from other employees, including her assistant, Megan Zamora, support the finding that Julianne has a reputation for bullying and threatening those who she feels are beneath her. Consequently, no one seemed willing to question her actions. We should probably do a review of policies and procedures and the current control structure. As SoJo continues to grow, the infrastructure of the company needs to evolve.

"Lastly, she rationalized the situation. In reviewing her oral and written statements, we see how Julianne justified her decisions. She indicated that a third party worked on the expense reporting process, therefore there are 'glitches' in the system. She goes on to say that she needs to stay at the St. Regis because it is close to Seibert Industries and she is required to entertain her clients. It is possible that she stayed elsewhere and rationalized billing the company for the higher expense covering the $700-per-night Fifth Avenue accommodations. Lastly, when talking about customer discounts, she indicated that discounts are received from raw material manufacturers, so offering a 30% discount off standard pricing is acceptable. Some of these facts I am not here to dispute; I'm just here to report what could have happened.

---

[4] https://www.acfe.com/fraud-triangle.aspx

"Brandon, I know you are reluctant to prosecute, but the evidence we have accumulated does lead us to believe additional discovery work is needed to rule out wrongdoing. To complete our investigation into kickbacks, we'd need to gather information from your customers. To finish piecing together the situation on her expense reports, we'd need transaction records from the St. Regis. That being said, much of Julianne's own statements indicate she is working very hard to mislead this investigation."

Brandon sat for a moment before saying, "I need to process this information. I appreciate the work you have done thus far. However, before we can proceed, we need to provide an update to the audit committee and the board. Kelli, I expect you to work with Dalton to pull the needed details together. Joseph, as our legal officer, I'd appreciate you running the hoops on governance. Please let me know if we need to call a special board meeting or if this matter can wait until we meet next month.

"Simon, I expect Julianne to remain on leave of absence until we have this sorted out. Please ensure you have connected with IT to limit her access to critical systems, customers, and records." Brandon stood and turned to Dalton. He shook his hand and said, "We will be in touch."

Kelli was as disappointed with the results as she was happy with the work Dalton and his team had completed. This was exactly what she was looking for. That is why she had reached out to Dalton: she knew she would get a professional investigation in addition to the myriad services she wanted to use him for. This was a great introduction to Dalton for Brandon. Kelli planned on suggesting that Brandon talk to Dalton on how to handle this situation moving forward.

CHAPTER THREE

Emotional Intelligence

D ALTON DRIVES INTO San Jose to meet with Stanton Electronics chief financial officer Brad Lester, a long-term friend and client. Dalton has his kids fly up and spend the weekend with Brad and his kids. Dalton takes in Dax's soccer game; Dax is Brad's eight-year-old and Brad is a vocal fan and demanding parent involved with the team. After the game, Dalton and Brad talk about Brad's impact on his son and how he can be intimidating in certain situations without realizing it. The conversation dovetails into the importance of empathy and how to use it effectively to build relationships and relate to people.

 ## PEOPLE-CENTRIC SKILLS IN THIS CHAPTER

- Emotional intelligence and why it is one of the most important skills of successful leaders
- Understanding emotions and how to manage them in the workplace
- Being self-aware and the importance of self-awareness in all situations
- The importance of empathy and the art of being truly emphatic

 ## KEY WORDS

- Emotional Intelligence
- Motivation

- Self-Reflection
- Self-Awareness

There's nothing like a late October Sunday morning—mid-50s, sunny, light breeze. Perfect weather for fútbol. Yes, perfect soccer weather. Caleb and Liora flew up Thursday night and Dalton and the kids spent Friday touring San Francisco and spent the weekend with Brad Lester. At the beginning of his career, Dalton worked for Brad at Arthur Andersen. Dalton always viewed Brad as a mentor. When Dalton started up his own business more than 10 years ago, he reached out to his circle of contacts and reconnected with Brad. Brad was the first person to use Dalton's organization for one very simple reason: he trusted Dalton. They had always had a strong relationship. When Brad went through some personal turmoil, Dalton was there for him. Both men were in good places, so this weekend was all about catching up and enjoying each other's company. Caleb's travel soccer team had a bye week so it was a perfect time to take a trip. Friday night had been perfect and everyone was up and out early to attend Dax's soccer game. Dax was eight and a pretty talented soccer player (from what Brad tells everyone).

One thing both families had in common is a strong affinity for soccer. Dalton played at a very competitive level as a kid and Brad played Division I soccer in college. Dalton pushed Caleb to soccer because of his size. Dalton, a stout six feet two inches, did not pass on his height to his son. Caleb was short, bordering on stocky, but the kid had great quickness and smarts and knew how to use the size he had. Dalton was always a physical athlete and that seemed to rub off on Caleb, who was a natural, picking up any sport quickly. He selected soccer and basketball as his focus. He joined a travel soccer team and has excelled and continued to grow. He is the team captain and center back; his coach does not take him off the field.

Dax seemed to be on a very similar progression to Caleb. This was his first year on a club soccer team. Brad coached him his first few years (and did not seem to want to give it up) but moved him to a club team once his skill level advanced. This was his first season with FC Strike and he was having a good year so far. He was the center midfielder, one of the key positions to overall team success. This morning, Strike was up against one of the better teams in the league, FC Bollingwood, sponsored by one of Great Britain's better professional teams.

The game was a tight one that Dalton and his kids enjoyed greatly. Even Liora—a pretty good goalie at one time although she did not play anymore—enjoyed watching the game (it was difficult to keep her attention on anything related to sports). With the game tied 1–1 at halftime, Brad was slowly but surely becoming more vocal. When Brad became stressed, he showed physical signs of being under pressure. He seemed to stress out more over Dax's soccer games than anything else. He did not live vicariously through his son, but he wanted him to be successful and put in maximum effort at all times. Dax was playing well but definitely not having his best game. He seemed bored or distracted. In fact, in the second half, Brad's cheering became more destructive and negative. The more he screamed, the less effort Dax seemed to give. The boys ended up losing 4–1.

FC Strikes' coach appeared upbeat about the loss and seemed to keep a positive message. Brad, on the other hand, was the opposite. He lost it with Dax; he did not necessarily yell but continued to question how hard Dax had played and why he didn't do this or that. Brad's wife, Candace, was irate with Brad, to the point that they had it out when they got home. Liora and Caleb took Dax to the loft in Brad's house to play video games until lunch and Dalton worked on calming Brad, and now Candace, down.

As they spent the afternoon relaxing and preparing dinner, they finally sat down to chat. After setting up drinks for everyone (Dalton with the standard vodka soda, Brad with the Scotch and soda, and Candace with a margarita on the rocks), they started to discuss this afternoon's game.

They went back through some of the handouts that Dalton had introduced Brad and his team to a few years back and reviewed them in detail. Dalton wanted to discuss emotional intelligence—not so casually—and how they were applying it with Brad's team. But he wanted to make sure he saw the parallels to Brad and Dax.

Emotional Intelligence

Emotional intelligence is a set of skills demonstrating the ability of an individual to recognize their behaviors, moods, and impulses, and to manage them best according to each unique situation.

Understanding the causes of emotions and how to use them to your advantage can help you to effectively identify who you are and how you interact best with others.

EQ Self-Appraisal

- Self-Management: Control of emotions, impulses, and adapting to changing circumstances

(continued)

- Self-Awareness: Awareness of one's emotions and recognizing their impact while using intuition to guide decisions
- Empathy: Ability to sense, understand, and react to others' emotions while comprehending social networks
- Self-Motivation: Staying focused in all critical situations; minimal dependency on others to motivate

Brad mentioned that he had been relatively successful applying this with his team. "We had every team member complete your EQ self-assessment and discuss some of their strengths and weaknesses. We spent three to six months applying the skills we identified were lacking." (See the appendix for the Emotional Intelligence Self-Assessment.)

Self-Management

Consistency: Stability/consistency is key to self-management. Constantly changing can cause others to question your beliefs and what you stand for and can also cause you to become confused about what you truly believe.

Stick to the plan: Do it right and in a timely way. Plans are made for a reason. Stick to them but be flexible as necessary. The goal is set; it must be met.

Be accountable: Things do not always work out as planned. That is normal, probably more normal than when they do work out. You have to be able to admit that and then use your flexibility to get things back on track. Flexibility is key; do not worry about it—move forward.

Educate yourself: Once we stop learning, we stop living and growth stagnates. Do not let change pass you by; embrace it. Read, read, and read some more. Talk and listen to mentors and peers; look for different perspectives. Once we stop evolving, we will be behind the times.

Stay mentally and physically fit: This is a very important part of being able to practice the other aspects of self-management. Exercising your body is just as crucial to self-management as exercising your mind. A body that is not well rested, nutritionally fed, or physically exercised can lead to emotional and physical illnesses.

Over the past few years, Brad has consistently improved upon these key points at work. He is anal-retentive and has a plan for everything. He is one of the most intelligent people Dalton knows but is always learning how to get better. Brad even holds himself accountable on everything—a true disciplinarian. He exercises his mind and his body and knows how much each means to his demeanor at the office. In fact, since Dax was born, Brad has even taken Dalton's lead and become a yogi, meditating nightly.

Self-Awareness

- Ability to perceive one's skills and knowledge accurately and realistically
- First step in the process of full acceptance or change
- Without understanding why one thinks or acts the way one does, they will never fully appreciate themselves or see the importance of making changes to improve, if necessary
- Gives power and a sense of peace/happiness

A lack of self-awareness can keep you from realizing your worth in the company or even the quality of the work you perform. This can have a serious impact on your personal and professional life. Not only will you have doubts about yourself, but the people you lead will also begin to question your competence, which could ultimately lead to a lack of leadership effectiveness.

In many respects, self-awareness came very naturally to Brad. When crossing a street, he tended to walk fast so cars wanting to turn right would be able to do so quickly. He enjoyed sitting in the back row of first class when flying because he thought it was very rude to lean his seat back into the person behind him. He was well aware of his surroundings. What Brad had discounted, in Dalton's opinion, was his impact on his son. Dax idolized his dad, like many boys do. As a dad, Brad understood his son looked up to him, but did not fully understand to what lengths.

Dalton asked Brad if Dax liked playing soccer. Because they respected each other, Brad tried to answer his question without emotion and as rationally as possible. He initially thought Dalton was attempting some of his very dry sarcasm. He answered, "D, I am surprised at your question. You know he likes playing soccer. No, scratch that. He *loves* playing soccer. He loves being on the field. He gets excited before every game. In fact, he is so excited before games that he throws up on occasion."

Dalton smiled. This was very similar to what he went through with his own son, Caleb. Caleb always got so nervous before games that he barely ate unless Dalton actually forced him to eat, and he has thrown up before and in the middle of games. His physical reaction was not from excitement but nerves. Caleb got stressed before games and has always been like this. For years, without Dalton realizing it, Caleb got stressed because he did not want to disappoint his father. After a few conversations, Caleb realized that the stress was still there but that this was stress for more positive reasons. He got stressed due to the level of competition; he wanted to do his best, and he did not want to let down his coach or teammates. The conversations Dalton had with Caleb about who he was and why he played soccer seemed to change Caleb's attitude toward the game. At times, he tended to appear burned-out and did not want to practice and could not get excited about games. Now, after understanding why he plays and who he plays for, he truly fell in love with the beautiful game again. He enjoyed practicing and pushing himself and his teammates. Dalton did not realize his son played soccer for him. The "ah-ha" moment was enlightening to him and his influence over his son.

Dalton explained this to Brad in great detail. Brad nodded and kept squinting his right eye and looking off into the distance. Dalton knew Brad well and had a baseline for his body language and facial expressions. When he saw this, he knew these were indicators that Brad was truly considering what was being presented to him. When Brad had already made up his mind and was not considering different views, he looked straight ahead at the speaker. He did not interrupt but he had a very stone-cold stare, because he was waiting for the person to be done talking and so he could rebut everything that was just said. Luckily, this was not one of those times.

Brad stated that he always told Dax, "I don't care if you play soccer or not, son. You play because you love the game, not for any other reason. I don't care if you play, but if you play, give it 110%. If you cannot do that, let's go back to rec soccer and just have fun." Again, the parallels between Dalton and Brad were endless. Dalton would say something to both Caleb and Liora about sports. It was meant to be a very positive, supportive message. One of his close friends and the young lady he has casually dated after his divorce, Meghan Dorsch, pointed out that the message could be misconstrued as a negative message. She pointed out that the kids might focus on the "I don't care" part versus the second, and more important, aspect of the statement. "They hear 'I don't care' versus the whole message. Why not tell them, 'Kids, you play sports for yourself and for your enjoyment and because you both are very good at it. You must have a passion for what you do. If you don't enjoy it, then I support your decision to quit and do something else. What I want you to do is understand why you play and play for the right reasons or stop playing for the right reasons.'"

One of Dalton's strongest personality traits is the open-mindedness and yearning to learn and being open to changing his perspective. This was one of those moments. That was why he enjoyed Meghan's company so much. He had learned that she was not only intelligent and beautiful but she always freely spoke her mind and she always brought a unique perspective to the table. He did not know if their relationship would ever advance past the stage of casually dating when Dalton was in town or vacationing once a year together, but he greatly enjoyed their time together and the kids took a liking to Meghan.

Dalton relayed this story to Brad and he appreciated the perspective. He definitely planned on having a similar discussion with Dax tomorrow because maybe Dax was hearing the wrong message as well.

Self-Regulation

- Ability to control one's emotions, desires, and behaviors in order to reach a positive outcome
- Art to finding the balance between expressing one's feelings and avoiding unnecessary tension

Self-Regulation is a direct reflection of the type of pressure one is experiencing. There is good and bad pressure:

1. Good: Result of an aggressive but nonharmful atmosphere. One views the people around them as an inspiration and uses this as motivation, which can lead to the acquisition of self-regulation.
2. Bad: When the atmosphere is critical and harmful. This pressure does not motivate and self-regulation is lost.

Brad worked extensively at self-regulation. He fostered a positive environment in the workplace and at home. In previous positions, he struggled with that because what he believed was a positive environment for him did not necessarily mean it was a positive environment for everyone. What Brad did not realize was that his atmosphere when it pertained to soccer for Dax was becoming toxic. Dax was emotionally immature, which was to be expected because he was a child. Fostering a positive environment enables Dax to continue to grow. On the other hand, fostering a critical atmosphere full of unnecessary tension can be harmful, stunting the growth of anyone at any age, especially a child.

Brad was a very positive thinker and utilized everything that was shown on the handout. He always stressed the importance of being an individual while still fitting together as puzzle pieces to form a team. He is very strong-willed and determined. With Dax, he might be pushing him too hard or for the wrong reasons.

Dalton and Brad then shifted the conversation to empathy, an area that Dalton was working on further developing himself. Empathy is the ability to share in the feelings of others, whatever those feelings are. Being able to share in an emotion—whether the extremes of joy or sadness or any other strong emotion—is an admirable trait. In order for empathy to work, a person must first be able to recognize, classify, and understand his own feelings.

Empathy is most useful when the one empathizing has experienced a variety of feelings. Empathy is not easy. People are not always forthcoming with problems, even when it is obvious that something is wrong. So people are forced to ask probing questions or read between the lines of what is said. Focusing on nonverbal cues is also a great way to read between the lines. Dalton's greatest growth area has been empathy and the ability to read people without them saying exactly what they are thinking.

Brad had actively learned how to be empathetic over the last few years, after he learned of its importance the hard way. Being a workaholic, Brad had let his career become more important than his wife, and his wife eventually left. As the main breadwinner in the family, Brad had held that over his wife. Not on purpose, but that was definitely how he made her feel, since she stayed home, working part-time and focusing on raising Dax and her daughters from her previous marriage. Brad was a wonderfully giving stepdad but Dalton always thought he resented the fact that the girls were not biologically his, even though he treated them as such.

Brad was not very empathetic to his wife and her struggles. She was a reasonably successful ad executive but always wanted to focus on raising her kids. Brad afforded her that opportunity. Over the years, Brad became consumed with his career, not because he particularly wanted to but because it was necessary based on his role. He never showed the appreciation Maria was looking for when she cooked and cleaned and took great care of the girls. He always felt that was her job. Maria was integrally involved with the girls and school, as homeroom mom and an active PTA leader. When Maria would talk about her volunteer activities, Brad would zone out or listen very passively and nod his head, merely acknowledging her with an "uh-huh." This would start many, many fights and periods of no communication. He told her on numerous occasions that he didn't really care if her work did not generate money. Dalton did not believe you could get less empathetic than that—he had made the same mistake himself. He never understood why his wife would not help him grow his business. She never had any interest and that always frustrated him—to the point that he began to resent all of her other efforts with volunteer works, religious education, and the rest. In many respects, Dalton and Brad were two peas in a pod.

Brad's life changed when he met Candace a few years after his divorce. In order to advance past controller to chief financial officer, he needed to improve on his communication and emotional intelligence. Dalton always said that people get promoted for the wrong reasons. Technical abilities and knowledge are integral, but without the ability to relate to and motivate people, success will be limited.

Candace had a great influence on Brad's personal and professional development. He listened to Candace. He respected Candace. She was blunt and honest with Brad, which was what he needed. He respects someone who is blunt and honest. Another reason why Brad and Dalton got alone so well was the blunt honesty each provided to the other.

Use Emotions to Facilitate Thinking

- How a person feels will determine how he or she views situations.
- This is also key when interpreting communications.
- Emotions can overwhelm the commonsense part of one's mentality.
- Negative conflict is driven by a lack of logical thinking.
- If emotions cloud thinking, it is very difficult to think straight and make sound decisions.
- Having control of your emotion and understanding when emotion clouds judgment leads to clear thinking and sound decision-making.

Dalton and Brad discussed this specifically in relation to handling Dax. Brad did not realize he was raising his voice or speaking angrily. He was so upset at the outcome of the games and how Dax played that it clouded his judgment. This was one of the few times that he did not self-regulate; he let his negative emotions control his reactions and thinking.

Gaining Control

- Control over yourself, your thoughts, and emotions is one of the most important aspects of emotional intelligence.
- Having control or the lack thereof could be the difference between building or destroying a successful career.

Using Coping Thoughts

When a situation arises that requires coping skills, try the following:

- Take a deep breath. Deep breathing has an amazing calming effect on the brain. By doing so, one can easily avoid the first, natural reaction to a stressful situation. This is key because the first reaction is usually an emotional, potentially irrational, and illogical reaction.
- Step away. Mentally take yourself away from the situation and analyze the issue itself, without the emotion. Easy to say, much harder to do. Ask the following questions:
  - Does this really matter?
  - Does it matter now?
  - Will it matter tomorrow? In one month? Ever again?
  - Does it truly impact me?
  - Am I allowing my emotions to override my rational thinking?
- Use positive thinking. Do not approach any situation with thoughts of anger, sadness, or other negative emotions. Think happy thoughts. This does not mean you are avoiding the problem, but rather is a way to prepare you to tackle it in a productive manner. Every problem has a potential solution.

In Dalton's classes, in this section, he always plays the scene from *Happy Gilmore,* where Happy's (Adam Sandler) grandmother tells him that she only wants him to be happy and go to his happy place in order to focus when under extreme duress. Regardless of the topic, Dalton always attempts to keep the subject light and fun. Adults learn more in fun, interactive environments. Dalton does in fact use this technique and uses it often—ever since he moved over from corporate America working for the "man" to focusing on training and coaching. It was very necessary that first year and has become an essential part of his routine. What is Dalton's happy place? There are many, but the most common scenarios involve the success of his kids (who, he truly believes, have unlimited potential), winning a big contract, or smiling when someone tells him that his training/coaching is truly life-changing. He imagines his son fulfilling his athletic and religious potential and his daughter at her first major success, whatever it will be (there are so many possibilities). One key aspect of positive imagery is what it does for you not only mentally but physically. Dalton has been known to get lost in his thoughts and begin to tear up from the positive imagery. Even more important is the smile this brings to his face. The power of a smile can change many situations. The power of a smile makes anyone approachable and can be infectious.

In addition to positive thinking and imagery, Dalton is a fanatical supporter of numerous coping mechanisms, including meditation and yoga. He constantly uses the breathing techniques he learned becoming a serious advocate of hot yoga, and this interest has allowed him to take on meditation, which has also become a ritual. That is something else that Brad and Dalton have in common: meditation.

Understand Emotions and How to Manage Them in the Workplace

- Understanding one's emotions and learning how to use them is the responsibility of each person.
- Can we ignore them? No—they are part of all of us and need to be used and understood and controlled appropriately.

(continued)

Example: You are a manager and your team is about to miss an important deadline. You can decide if you should get stressed and what level of stress is appropriate to how necessary it is for you to meet the deadline. There are numerous options, so you need to decide which makes sense for you and, more importantly, for the team:

- Call a team meeting and explain the ramifications of not meeting the deadline.
- Yell and scream and tell the team they have to meet the deadline no matter what.
- Make a mandatory 24/7 workday to meet the deadline.
- Don't worry about the deadline and let it play out.

This would also be a good time to listen to the team members to find out if there is something out of their control that is preventing them from doing their job.

The first option seems to be the most rational. A less calm and more volatile method would be to yell at everyone and tell them to get to work. Deciding which style is best can be done by weighing the pros and cons of each as well as which would result in the most positive outcome. Do not rely solely on how you feel, but on what makes logical sense.

Dalton has always joked that he is dead inside. "This is what my wife tells me!" he would state emphatically when he was married. He was only partially kidding; Dalton's father told him that being emotional was not what men do. He saw the negative outcomes from unmanaged emotion when his father would have uncontrollable outbursts for no other reason than a bad day at work. His father did not get physical with Dalton and his brothers often, but when he did, it was always memorable. What scarred the boys more was the mental abuse. The screeching of their father's voice, belittling them and making them feel worthless. That was always in the back of Dalton's mind. In fact, a driving factor in Dalton's success was his father, not to win his father's approval but more to stick it to his dad that he was going to be successful in spite of his father.

Dalton was not an emotional man, but something did click 12 years ago, when he started having kids. It was like an emotional switch was turned on inside of him, not for everything, but for anything related to his kids. When Caleb (and subsequently Liora, who is 11) was born, he could not get through a kid movie without tearing up. In fact, the kids have a completely different opinion of Dalton. They perceive him as an emotional wreck who cries at all movies (for many years, the only movies Dalton saw were kid movies). As a longtime season ticket holder, he also had a huge weak spot for the Dallas Mavericks, his team. The Mavericks were the proverbial black sheep of the National Basketball Association (NBA) during the 1990s. The talent base improved and, surprisingly, the Mavericks were the NBA champions in 2010–11. Dalton vividly tells the story of the clinching game, which he could not attend because he was speaking at a large fraud conference. He watched game six at the hotel bar and, once they clinched, was overcome with emotion. He held it together until he got up to his hotel room and proceeded to cry uncontrollably while watching the celebration for the next three hours. It was a true release of many years of pent-up frustration and emotion. To this day, whenever his kids try to manipulate him, they turn on the Mavericks championship video and Dalton still tears up!

Other than these obvious weaknesses, he was a rock. Yet he realizes how important emotions are in the workplace and how challenging it is to use your emotions in a productive way. If you do not understand how people work and what drives or motivates someone, you will never get the best out of anyone. He has applied this theory with his son Caleb.

Caleb is a highly skilled soccer player who plays in a top youth league in the United States. At 12, he has a great opportunity to do something special. It has been a long journey. Five years ago, Caleb had an indoor soccer game during the summer. He was not playing at a high level. At best he was doing okay. He just did not seem to be putting in a lot of effort. At every game, Caleb would ask Dalton for his rating, on a simple 1–10 scale, with 10 meaning great and 1 meaning awful. Dalton was very positive in most cases, trying to continue to motivate Caleb through the power of positivity. In this instance, due to some extenuating factors and the lack of effort he had witnessed during the game, Dalton was not his positive self. He pondered how to approach this and thought it best to discuss once they got home and were less emotional. As soon as Caleb got in the car, he seemed concerned. He asked his dad for his score and—in the most positive way he could, considering the circumstances—Dalton replied that they could chat about it later. Not one to let things go, Caleb began to cry because he knew what Dalton's avoidance of the topic meant.

After a tense car ride home, Dalton sat down with Caleb and calmed him down. Dalton told him that he was very proud of all of his accomplishments and that he was extremely talented and much more accomplished at the beautiful game than his father. Dalton sat eye to eye with Caleb, to make sure he knew this was coming from a place of love.

"Caleb, I do not have a rating for you for the game. I honestly did not know when you were on the field. You did not do anything positive to impact the game and you did not do anything negative to impact the game. You did not do much at all."

By now, Caleb was quietly sobbing. Dalton continued. "Buddy, I am not mad at you. I am not disappointed in you. I love you very much. I always want to be honest with you so we can work through things together." This seemed to calm him down.

"Bubba, did you give your best effort?" Dalton asked. Caleb responded unsurely, "I think so." Dalton reminded him how much he loved watching him play and how he knew how good he could be. He said that, in his opinion, he knew Caleb could do more.

"The only thing you can control, Buddy, is your effort. You are going to mess up. You are going to be tired, sick, mad, sad, and everything else. When you are on that field, the one thing you can always do is give it your everything. Always walk off that field proud!"

One of Dalton's favorite quotes is from former President Calvin Coolidge: "Nothing in this world can take the place of persistence. Talent will not; nothing is more common than unsuccessful men with talent. Genius will not; unrewarded genius is almost a proverb. Education will not; the world is full of educated derelicts. Persistence and determination alone are omnipotent."

Dalton would constantly quote this to his kids in a more modern fashion: "The Zimmers are not the smartest nor the most athletic people in the world. But if you outwork everyone, you will be successful."

The conversation continued and Caleb promised he would give more effort, for his dad. Dalton almost lost it when he heard this.

"Caleb, if you are playing for me, then we need to revisit what we are doing here. Buddy, you should never do this for me. You play for your teammates. You play because you love it. You play for yourself. If you do not want to play, that's fine."

This conversation helped Caleb refocus and continue to excel at soccer. In order to refocus his efforts, Dalton had to put himself in his son's shoes to really understand what motivated him. He craved his father's approval but needed to look internally to find his true passion and strength.

The Role of Emotional Intelligence at Work

Emotional intelligence plays a vital role in the workplace. How one feels about oneself, interacts with others, and handles conflict is directly reflected in the quality of work produced. The more confident and "bought-in" an employee is, the better the product that will be produced. Social proficiencies are developed as a result of emotional intelligence.

Social Proficiencies

Empathy: Being aware of others' feelings and exhibiting compassion. Truly making an effort to understand why someone feels the way they do.

Intuition: An inner sense of the feelings of others. Understanding others without asking about others. A general feeling of how another's behavior is communicated through nonverbal cues.

Political Acumen: Ability to communicate, strong influence and leadership skills, and conflict resolution.

Both Dalton and Brad had progressively become very good at empathy and intuition. In their 20s, both men had been somewhat clueless about both topics. But through many life events, they matured emotionally.

For many years, Dalton thought most people surrounding him in corporate America did not work hard. His father's workday was consistently 6–6 throughout his youth. When Dalton's employees told him they had to leave early to pick up their kids, or some other personal reason, he thought they were not dedicated. Until he had Caleb and Liora, he did not understand what motivated people. He did not understand how to push people to do more; he thought having a job was enough motivation for anyone. Once he developed a relationship with his employees and understood why they were working and what truly motivated them, he became a respected and successful leader. By understanding others and showing true empathy, Dalton began to relate to anyone and everyone.

This also led Dalton to a higher level of intuition. As much as he wished he had this during his marriage, intuition and empathy assisted Dalton in having a true friendship with his ex-wife, and in understanding his daughter and what she was beginning to go through (puberty).

Brad was viewed as a straightforward, straitlaced rule follower throughout his career. He was well-respected but ruled through fear. If you crossed him, there would be hell to pay. Dalton and Brad had gotten along and become good friends due to the straightforward nature of Brad's communication, but he was not known as someone who was emotionally intelligent or empathetic. He believed in black and white, not gray. It was either one way or the other—there were no other answers. In reality, there are many circumstances that could impact any situation. As Brad advanced to chief financial officer (in many respects, the culmination of his long career), he had to evolve as a leader. The largest piece of this evolution was not to attempt to treat all of his employees the same; he had learned that each person is unique and must be treated as such in order to maximize performance. This helped him transform from a good leader to a great leader.

Disagreeing Constructively

- Means to do so in a positive, productive manner.
- Purpose is not to disagree to get your point across.
- Not used to be negative or destructive of another's ideas.
- Workplace disagreement is a common occurrence.
- Companies look for the most effective ways to carry out operations and therefore invest in process improvement strategies, which opens the floor for discussion and compromise.
- Constructive disagreement acknowledges and confirms another's ideas before presenting your own.

Dalton consistently stresses to clients that anything can be said to anyone and it can be done from a positive point of view. The perfect example of this is when discussing high-risk clients. Instead of saying "high-risk," which might offend a client, state that the client is important to the overall success of the organization. The important thing is to give a simple, positive take on the message. Phrases such as "I disagree," "You are wrong," and "That is way off-base" quickly drive any person to become defensive.

The dissolution of his marriage had taught Dalton about the importance of communication. They had stopped communicating during the months leading up to their separation and divorce. This lack of communication made each of them spite each other, instead of appreciating each other more. When they did talk, it was more light shouting and emotionally driven. Dalton firmly believes that if they had each understood the other's point of view and if communication hadn't stopped, they would still be together.

Dalton and Brad spoke about using this knowledge not only in the workplace but at home and, specifically, with Dax. Dalton suggested that Brad not argue with him but hear him out. Discuss; do not dissent. Understand his perspective more. They paused when they realized they would overcook their dinner if they did focus on the grill!

CHAPTER FOUR

Different Points of View: Using Self-Awareness and Empathy Effectively

THE NEXT DAY, after Dalton's conversation with Brad on emotional intelligence and how to apply it in the workplace and at home, Brad applies these key learnings on an important conversation with his son, Dax.

PEOPLE-CENTRIC SKILLS IN THIS CHAPTER

- How to use empathy to build strong relationships
- Being self-aware and the importance of self-awareness in all situations
- The art of being truly empathic and its importance

KEY WORDS

- Emotional Intelligence
- Motivating Others
- Self-Reflection
- Self-Awareness

Brad, Candace, Dalton, and the kids had a great dinner at Brad's place, under the beautiful view of the sun bowing down behind the mountains. All the adults stayed and chatted over many rounds of drinks while the kids played video games and then watched a movie and fell asleep in the loft. Brad went to bed riddled with guilt, coming to the realization that he might be the cause of Dax's stress.

Dax was truly a blessing in his life. Due to a severe accident as a teenager, Brad was physically unable to have kids. Maria and Brad tried but time and time again, they were told it would be a fruitless effort and that was proven correct. Brad was 41 and Candace 43 when she began to experience morning sickness. She went to the gynecologist and they joked about whether she was pregnant. The miracle occurred and they were blessed with Dax.

The next morning, Brad woke Dax up early and took him to breakfast at their favorite hole-in-the-wall restaurant, The Café. He enjoyed the beauty of a simplistic name, like those places that are only named "DONUTS."

Dax was still at a young enough age that he liked to dress like his dad. Both had on their Adidas Firebird tracksuits, Brad in all black and Dax in all white. This was also a personal favorite look of Dalton's. The morning was cool, bordering on cold. Fall in San Jose always brought great swings in temperatures throughout the day.

Brad ordered the omelet with wheat toast and Dax went for the Nutella pancakes. Dax was always very happy to spend alone time with his dad, especially the early mornings. Both were early risers and loved to get out before everyone else.

After enjoying breakfast for a while, Brad broached the topic of yesterday's game. He started with a simple apology.

"Son, I wanted to apologize to you about how I acted yesterday."

"It's okay, Dad. It's no big deal." Dax really did not want to have this conversation and potentially spoil a great morning with his dad. "Dax, I want you to know that I just want you to be happy. I love watching you play soccer; you really are fantastic. If you don't want to play or enjoy playing, that is okay. You are still my boy and I will always love you whatever you do." Dax rarely saw his dad speak with this level of emotion.

Dax told him, "Dad, I love soccer. It makes me happy, and I am good at it. Sometimes, I get tired of playing. I still love it but it is a lot at times."

Even at eight, Dax had an intense schedule. Practice two nights a week, for two hours a night, and games every weekend, year-round.

Brad continued, "Buddy, if it is too much for you, then we can back off. You did commit to your teammates, so I think we should finish out this season and then talk about it then. Will that work for you? Again, Buddy, I love you and I want you to be happy."

Dax paused for a minute and considered what his father had said. He knew this was tough for his dad. He believed his dad but he also loved soccer. Soccer made him happy. His dad made him happy. He did not want to quit soccer.

"Dad, I love soccer. I don't want to quit. If you could let me play and not yell, I think that would help." This was an important step for Dax—giving his dad some candid feedback.

Brad smiled brightly, knowing last night's conversation with Dalton was very productive. "Dax, my man, I will do my best not to say anything through-out the game. The only thing I can ask of you is that if you do play, always give 111% effort. You can't control if you are having a bad game but you can con-trol your effort. If you always give a great effort, everything else will work itself out."

Dax smiled, knowing this was a consistent message from his dad. "Deal!" he shouted empathically, as they both repeated the message out loud:

"Good players give 110%. Great players give 111!"

Dalton and Dax headed home, bellyes and hearts full. Once they pulled into the driveway, Dalton was playing basketball with Caleb as Liora looked on. Dax jumped out of the car and jumped right into the game. Dalton and Brad made eye contact but nothing really needed to be said. Brad smiled brightly, silently stating, without words, *thank you*. Dalton smiled and watched the boys shoot together.

Brad dropped Dalton and the kids off at Norman Y. Mineta San Jose Inter-national Airport, and everyone said their goodbyes. Dax was already missing Caleb and Liora before they even left. Being an only child, he was always excited to see kids he looked up to and has known since their birth and it was a big let-down when they left. Dalton gave Candace a warm hug and did the same to Brad, knowing they would see each other again very soon.

CHAPTER FIVE

Wrong Mode = Wrong Mood: Determining the Optimal Mode of Communication

D ALTON'S EX-WIFE is Caleb's newly appointed soccer team manager and wants to make sure the communication issues that the team has suffered from in the past do not continue to occur. Over dinner, Leslie and Dalton discuss some situations that have developed and how they should have been communicated.

PEOPLE-CENTRIC SKILLS IN THIS CHAPTER

- Pros and cons of each mode of communication
- What the ramifications are of choosing the wrong mode of communication
- What mode of communication to use in any situation?

KEY WORDS

- Communication Mode
- Emotional Communication

Dalton and the kids arrived home after the long flight back to Dallas. They were unpacking as Leslie came over to help and to take them over to her place, a few miles away. Leslie was in a very chipper mood, joking around with the kids and being very complimentary to Dalton. He knew this was out of the normal. Ever since their separation and subsequent divorce, Leslie was usually very cold and impersonal around Dalton. They had a good relationship but Leslie was not outwardly friendly towards him. She tried to mask her frustration and disappointment with the situation but she could not; it was not something she was good at. She wore her emotions openly. Dalton was far from a perfect father and even farther from a perfect spouse, but he worked hard now to make this work. This was reality; there was no escaping the fact that they were divorced and that it would be tough on the kids. Living in reality was key; you have to deal with the situation at hand.

It was nice to see Leslie happy but he knew this meant she wanted something. Eventually, the ask would come. As Leslie packed up the kids and loaded everyone into her black Escalade, she asked Dalton very casually if he would like to come by and join them for dinner. Dalton did not have to say anything; he looked her with his hands on his hips, head turning sideways (chin to the left), and furrowed his brow. He did not say anything but he said a lot. Leslie jumped in, "I know, I know. I really need your advice and help on something. I was asked to take over as Caleb's soccer team manager and I want to get your thoughts on some initial first steps." Dalton smiled because he was excited that this had happened. Leslie was very good with people and this was something the team sorely needed. The other team manager did a great job but he was very busy with his actual job and was not as hands-on as necessary at times. Dalton pushed Leslie to take on this role, so this was a very good thing. Dalton was happy with this development and although he wanted to stay in and clean up and get ready for the week, he happily agreed to come over for dinner.

Dalton threw on his Adidas tracksuit and headed over to Leslie's a little before six. They were very casual and ordered Chinese takeout (Leslie was not one to cook much). Dinner was pleasant as the kids filled in their mother about their weekend in San Jose. Leslie had always liked Brad and was happy he was doing well. The kids ran upstairs after dinner, Liora to read and watch YouTube and Caleb to play NBA 2K20, which had just come out on Xbox.

Dalton and Leslie sat down with coffee and chatted about her new role. They both played revisionist historian, discussing some of the missteps with Caleb's teams in the past. At one time, the parents had major problems with his coach, Coach Steven. Steven was a yeller, and at first he appeared to be a motivator—a positive yeller. That was one of the reasons Caleb joined the team; Dalton thought it would help push Caleb to greater heights. They figured out very quickly that they had made a big mistake. After one season with Steven and continual bad play, no improvement from Caleb, and constant belittling regardless of whether the kids did something good or not, it was time for a change.

The team manager, Jon, sent out an email about a team meeting for the next week; Dalton and Leslie were out of town and could not make it. Jon sent out a summary of the meeting and asked for parents' opinions on Steven. What happened over the next four hours was a ridiculous email exchange—a perfect example of choosing the wrong mode of communication. Dalton was speaking all day at a conference and saw over fifty messages from parents about Steven, some for and some against. He was baffled that adults would communicate in this manner.

Dalton firmly believes that the right mode of communication drives good communication. When picking the right mode, regardless of what is communicated, anything can be communicated effectively. If the wrong mode is chosen, there is an increased chance of confrontation, regardless of how simplistic or controversial the message being communicated is.

The next morning, Dalton emailed Jon a one-sentence message: "Jon, do you have a few minutes to chat regarding your message?" They spoke on the phone and Dalton passed along his thoughts. Within two months, Caleb left the team (Caleb told Dalton he was scared of Steven and Caleb was not a kid who scares easily). The miscommunication continued and the situation actually ended with badly handled conflict. Dalton was out of town so he reached out to Steven by phone to tell him Caleb was leaving the team. Caleb was not a favorite of Steven's and he was not playing much by the end. Steven did not answer his phone, so Dalton left a voicemail and texted him three times that day to chat. Even though Dalton believed that email was the wrong mode of communication in this instance, he was left with no choice but to email Steven to let him know that Caleb was leaving the team and the reasons why. Time was of the essence and Steven had refused to respond. In fact, Steven never responded to the voicemail, making an already bad situation worse. Postscript: Coach Steven no longer coaches boys' youth soccer; all of his players left for similar reasons.

Dalton and Leslie laughed now; their time with Coach Steven appeared comical in retrospect. They had come a long way since then. On Caleb's last team, Dalton and Leslie shared duties and that seemed to work. Dalton was the long-term planner, working on getting a calendar of games and practices and tournaments to everyone nine months to one year in advance. Leslie was the people person (ironic, to say the least, considering her behavior toward Dalton and the fact that he was the public speaker in the family) and she handled all of the day-to-day. They discussed splitting this role up in a similar manner with this new team.

Dalton knew Leslie would ask about mode of communication and types of communication because this was something she struggled with at times. In fact, they discussed a parent of a boy on the team who was not the greatest communicator. Tiffany would send abrasive messages via WhatsApp. Every time she was not happy with something going on with the team (which was most of the time), she made sure to tell everyone. As soon as she messaged something negative, everyone knew there would eventually be a follow-up apology or motivational statement ("Let's not worry about this; we are here for the boys."). After chatting with her a few times and seeing her communication methods, Dalton knew she was a cancer on the team and both he and Leslie steered clear of her as much as possible.

Tiffany is an example of the classic social media bully: very bold and aggressive in social media and messaging but someone who cowers in person. Due to her poor communication skills, Dalton was not the only one who labeled her a cancer. Many of the other parents just stayed away from her as much as possible and disengaged. The worst part was that Dalton believed it had begun to reflect on her son. When considering her son for next year's team, Dalton knew the coach would question if the kid was good enough to offset having to deal with his mother. That is truly shameful.

Dalton discussed with Leslie how to choose the right mode of communication. People choose the wrong mode of communication all of the time. Dalton firmly believed that the root cause of this issue is the innate fear of conflict. People choose the easy way instead of the right or proverbial hard way. In fact, Dalton had dated a woman named Brooke for three months, and the relationship ended with the wrong mode of communication.

When at a speaking engagement and this topic was discussed, Dalton always asked if anyone in the class had broken up with someone via text. There were almost always a few people in class who had done so. If the relationship was at all meaningful, Dalton would ask how this person reacted to the breakup text. Every person stated that it had not gone well and that the other person in the relationship continued to call or text after the breakup. Dalton found it comical that the person who did the breaking up thought the other person was weird for reacting this way. Dalton would mention the fact that since it was a meaningful relationship and they disrespected the other person by not breaking up in person, this caused the aggressive reaction.

Brooke and Dalton dated for a short period; Brooke lived in Chicago so they only saw each other periodically and Dalton made his priorities clear for the time being: kids, career, kids. That would eventually change but that was best for now. Brooke struggled with this and had planned to end her relationship with Dalton (if you could call it that). Instead of calling Dalton or even texting to tell him the reasons, she, in fact, ghosted him. To Dalton, ghosting was a new concept: the practice of suddenly ending all contact with a person without explanation, especially in a romantic relationship.[1] Dalton was traveling to Chicago and they had planned dinner but he never heard from her again. He was actually concerned for her safety but figured out what happened through social media. He did not text more than a few times the evening dinner was planned. The final text he sent said, "I am sorry this did not work out for you. You are a wonderful person and I only wish you the best." He found Brooke's ghosting a sign of extreme immaturity and disrespect to the relationship they had. Leslie laughed when she heard this story, particularly since Dalton was more than 15 years older than Brooke!

Dalton and Leslie continued to discuss the best modes of communication, which is very much based on what is being communicated, the situation, and the type of communication. In general, the main modes of communication are:

- In person
- Phone
- Email
- Text/instant message

The mode of communication selected should be based on specific communication criteria (see Figure 5.1):

- **Emotion:** Direct correlation between the level of emotion driven by the communication and the more personal nature of the mode of communication (in-person)
- **Urgency:** Indirect correlation between the speed of communication and the personal nature of the communication
- **Dialogue:** Direct correlation between the level of discussion/dialogue necessary and the more personal nature of the mode of communication (in-person/phone)

---

[1] https://www.dictionary.com/e/ghosting/

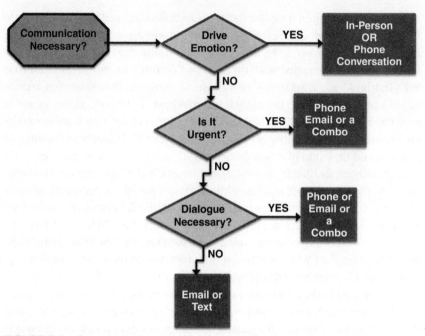

FIGURE 5.1   Communication Mode Selection Chart.

Dalton had tried to create a catchy acronym based on this list (Mode of Communication is DUE) but thought it was of utmost urgency to keep them in order based on importance. For example, if your communication will drive emotion and is urgent, *do not* default to email because of the speed or ease of communication. What we all must learn about email is that *sending* the email does not complete your communication; our message needs to be acknowledged/accepted by the other party. The intent of the communication is not met by sending the email. Tiffany broke this rule on a daily basis. She would send texts that were very emotionally driven and condescending. In fact, she had recently sent one in reaction to a miscommunication (that had frustrated everyone) with "SMH," which is shorthand for "shaking my head." This is very condescending. If she was frustrated with the situation, she should have emailed the team manager only and expressed her frustration in a constructive manner. Instead, this was done for everyone to see.

It seemed as if Leslie was about to respond jokingly with "SMH" after Dalton pulled out the decision chart he had created. She was laughing because this was quintessential Dalton. It was one of the reasons she fell in love with him and also why he annoyed the heck out of her!

Dalton was in teaching mode. "The decision chart is important for everyone when they communicate; however, once you have a strong working relationship with another person, the rules can be bent, potentially. The rules go out the window and you learn each other's communication style. I strongly believe that some rules should not be broken—such as that emotional communication should not be done over text or email—but again, you adjust to each other's preferences. I think we adjusted to each other's preferences over time, but we also did not adhere to good communication protocol as much as we should have."

Leslie reluctantly agreed. Dalton applied his "rules" all the time and Leslie firmly believed that rules cannot be applied at times. She was emotionally driven and she needed closure immediately, but she realized that can be very unhealthy.

Dalton and Leslie discussed the tendency toward the more impersonal forms of communication, email and text. Dalton has emoji-only conversations with his mom and even has lengthy conversations via text with clients—he never thought that would happen!

Still in teaching mode, Dalton continued. "The main consideration needs to be the level of miscommunication that can occur with these impersonal modes. People tend to read emotion into texts and emails, which sometimes leads to miscommunication. Make sure impersonal communication is emotionally clear and neutral, which should lessen the chance of misinterpretation. If you are not sure if it is clear, do not send it!"

Remember, the mode of communication might be even more important than what you are communicating in the first place. Pick the wrong mode and watch the effectiveness and efficiency of your communication spiral out of control. Even if it is difficult and more time-consuming, picking the right mode will help alleviate consternation and conflict.

CHAPTER SIX

Influencing Change Throughout Any Business

D ALTON DELIVERS ONE of his signature courses on how to look for deficiencies and continually improve any business process. He starts the presentation with the importance of communication throughout any organization, highlighting the foundation of a successful corporate culture: transparent, continuous communication.

PEOPLE-CENTRIC SKILLS IN THIS CHAPTER

- The importance of transparent communication when building trust
- How often, with whom, and when to communicate during change management
- Ramifications of not communicating effectively
- Combatting Natural Reactions to Change

KEY WORDS

- Influence
- Change Management
- Transparent Communication
- Continuous Communication

- Corporate Silos
- Building Resiliency

This was a rare treat for Dalton. Treats are all relative, so while sitting in Dallas traffic was never a treat, the ability to drive to work was, without a doubt, a treat. Additionally, the ability to drive his car for a few days was a rare treat, indeed. He had recently turned in his leased Lexus LS 460 for a brand-new Kia Telluride. He loved his Lexus but the Kia was very nice and he needed more space when driving the kids and taking Caleb to his out of town soccer games.

Today, Dalton was driving downtown to a new client who had found him through referrals from other clients. Dalton's business was very dependent on referrals and he was extremely thankful for a strong, loyal client base. Through the 55-minute drive that, without traffic, should have taken 25 minutes, Dalton thought through the day's presentation. He would be speaking about how to influence change throughout any business. It was not a full-day presentation (his specialty) just two hours. This did not require much preparation but he did think through the angle he would take to garner the group's attention.

This was an all-hands meeting for a large technology company that was growing rapidly. In fact, the founder, Barry Silverstein, was concerned that the company was outgrowing its infrastructure—not only its information technology infrastructure but also its cultural infrastructure. For the first few years, Barry's team was a tight-knit, small group. Then the app they created took off and they entered rapid expansion. Now Barry had to hire a bunch of outsiders due to the speed of the expansion and he knew the company culture had to evolve. Yet it was changing slower than the company's expansion. Barry was hopeful that Dalton could come in and establish some baselines for the team to adhere to as the company continued to grow. Barry did not know Dalton in a professional sense but they had known each other for years because they were congregants at the same synagogue. Barry was always impressed with Dalton and what he had been able to accomplish over the past 10 years. One of Barry's team members mentioned that they had attended many of Dalton's presentations in the past and Barry connected the dots from there. This was the first time he had engaged anyone like this in this capacity.

Dalton arrived and set up in the main conference room (with a capacity of 500) for his nine am session. Everyone filed in and began to settle a few minutes after the scheduled time. For the shorter sessions—especially the ones that were in town, where he had access to his full wardrobe—he enjoyed dressing up as part of a strong first impression. Today he wore his light brown three-piece suit, lightly patterned with blue houndstooth. He accentuated the suit with a blue shirt and navy blue tie and finished it off with dark brown and white wingtips.

Dalton wanted to attract the attention of the group with a strong opening message. He liked to personalize each presentation and so he thought of a personal yet universal message. He spoke of his own life changes and how he has had to change with the times rather than work against them, because change is inevitable. He talked about how difficult the transition was for the kids and even for him. His continuing message to the kids and even to his ex has been that this is inevitable, and that it will be better for everyone long-term. A tough message, but everything was falling into place for both the kids and the adults. In fact, both kids had noticed how much more pleasant their parents were to be around.

Barry worked with Dalton to help to define the change management strategy that DCL Technologies was planning to use. Dalton introduced the strategy blueprint to the company via PowerPoint. Key components introduced included the following.

Strategy Component	Company-Specific Message
Description of the proposed change vision, and its goals	Evolve the business processes, technology, and culture at DCL as we continue to grow over the next five years.
Reasons why the change is necessary	We expect significant growth over this time. We must evolve the organization or face significant disruption in our strategy and ability to recruit top personnel.
Critical success measures and key performance indicators	▪ Project needs for business processes, technology, and culture for the next five or more years ▪ Perform gap analysis for each ▪ Determine critical needs for each ▪ Change management team to track progress for each
Project stakeholders and stakeholder groups and their involvement	▪ Senior management ▪ Change champions ▪ Everyone!
Key messages to communicate	See above

Dalton played the role of communicator and motivator perfectly. Barry needed the whole team to be on board with the fact that status quo did not work anymore. Dalton needed to motivate and convince the organization this was the right direction to go. He enjoyed presentations like this; Barry was there to jump in and support and reiterate the message. Without that additional voice, the task at hand would be much more difficult.

Dalton continued and reiterated the change and why DCL must evolve to make sure everyone had a clear understanding of the overall nature of the change, its reasons, and how it would align with the vision for DCL. He outlined the risks of not changing, timing for the change, and who would be most impacted by the change.

Barry thought this was the perfect role for Dalton, an outsider, to communicate. He wanted everyone to understand that change is constant in this environment and understanding its components can help everyone relate it to an organizational level. He also wanted them to know that senior management understood its impact on the individual because change influences all levels of the organization. Organizational change creates fear and uncertainty, and Barry wanted to get ahead of this as much as possible.

Dalton walked the team through the five natural reactions to change experienced by employees:

1. **Denial:** May be reluctant to listen or may deny any facts or information presented to support the change if they are not informed in a timely manner or are told of things after the fact.
2. **Resistance:** This common reaction stems from fear of the unknown.
3. **Anger:** When change occurs and the norm is disturbed, people can experience anger. They may lash out and become uncooperative during this time.
4. **Indifference:** People may just not care, or the change may appear not to have an impact on their routines or work. Be wary of this: the change may be intended to have an impact, but if the individual is indifferent about the change, then he or she may not understand or accept it.
5. **Acceptance:** Changes occur for the better and have a positive influence on those involved. Even with positive change, acceptance may not happen right away but should occur more quickly, as opposed to when the change is perceived to be negative.

Dalton walked everyone through these reactions and then opened up a Q and A session for Barry and other members of the senior management team to field questions. They did their best to focus on keeping an open atmosphere and did field some good questions, but they also knew that the people who were truly in denial or indifferent would most likely not ask questions in this open environment. Again, it was a good opportunity to begin to clear the air on where DCL was moving.

The remainder of Dalton's presentation focused on building flexibility and resiliency, but he wanted to do this by tapping into the emotional side of the team. He wanted to get them to fully buy-in and get excited about where DCL had been and where it is heading. Dalton was not an emotional person but he knew the importance of emotion and getting employees emotionally attached to the company message and mission statement.

Dalton dove into the topic of resiliency and how to build it as a foundational piece of DCL moving forward.

Resiliency is the ability to recover from or adjust easily to misfortune or change.[1] It is not a personality characteristic in itself; rather, it is a combination of traits. Dalton walked through these traits with great passion as he saw many of these traits in himself and his kids. He loved the quote (he never said it correctly) about how bad things happen but it's best to focus on your reaction and how you bounce back rather than playing the victim. Caleb used to have many minor injuries in soccer and was always very slow to recover. Dalton always pushed him to power through these things, believing it was not the injury itself but how quickly someone can recover from the injury that matters. Over the past year, Caleb became resilient and powered through most anything.

Dalton highlighted the importance of being resilient. When people are confronted with ambiguity and loss of control, they tend to gain from such experiences rather than lose. They thrive when faced with chaos. Dalton was a very routine-oriented person but loved the thought of applying the chaos theory in life. He knew that life does not go the way you plan and preparing for the unexpected is key. In fact, his career and company arose from utter chaos in his life. He would call out Caleb and Liora when they were too risk averse and never took chances. He would talk to Caleb about using controlled aggression and not thinking so much on the soccer field, and instead just doing. Liora would stress over school all the time and he constantly reminded her that stress can be a self-fulfilling prophecy. Stress caused her to get bad grades on occasion. Whenever she came home with a grade she was not happy with, he told her not to focus on the grade but on how she got the grade and how they could make sure this did not happen again.

He relayed these stories with great passion and reverence. His kids were his everything, and anybody who heard Dalton speak knew that. Resilient people are more likely to make a quicker and more effective adaptation to change. Resilient people are necessary to foster success during a change.

Dalton introduced integral steps to help employees and leaders become more resilient:

1. Have a realistic picture of your capabilities but do not limit yourself.
   a. Realism is the key to growth. However, realism should not be a limitation.

---

[1] https://www.merriam-webster.com/dictionary/resilience

2. Have no fear of failure, but instead embrace failure as a learning opportunity.
   a. The world today is full of participation trophies.
   b. Losing = Learning
   c. Every great leader has failed at some point!
3. Embrace risk-taking.
   a. Inherent in every risk is an opportunity.
4. Concentrate on continuing to develop critical-thinking skills (think outside the box).
   a. Focus on new approaches for everything.
   b. Continue to reinvent yourself.
   c. If you are in the middle of a change, suspend immediate judgment.
5. Embrace detailed, regimented project management throughout the organization.
   a. Use a planner or planning software to keep to-do lists, and track plans, commitments, and next steps for each change initiative.
   b. Break down complex or ambiguous situations into manageable chunks.
   c. Find a coach who has strong organizational skills.
6. Maintain focus on long-term goals and objectives but be flexible.
   a. Reassess goals and objectives periodically.

Barry reiterated some of these key messages and Dalton started to wrap up with the importance of flexibility. Being flexible is critical for people involved in or leading a change to be able to make shifts as necessary during a project. Flexible people are team players, a critical need for any change management initiative. Flexibility allows one to think with an open mind and brainstorm more efficiently, which helps to bring a wider range of ideas to a project team.

Dalton was very good at his craft but on rare occasions, a presentation did not go as well as he wanted. Luckily, this was not one of those times. Dalton could call out the highs and lows and this was a major high. He read the attendees' faces over the two hours and kept coming back to Barry. Dalton could see the enthusiasm and excitement on his face and hear it on his voice. As Dalton wrapped up with a strong final message, the team rose and gave him a standing ovation, which was truly a highlight for Dalton. He stuck around for lunch and chatted with the executive team about continued assistance throughout the next year. He left excited about the possibilities.

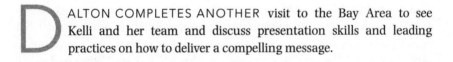

CHAPTER SEVEN

Projecting the Real You: Public Speaking

D ALTON COMPLETES ANOTHER visit to the Bay Area to see Kelli and her team and discuss presentation skills and leading practices on how to deliver a compelling message.

PEOPLE-CENTRIC SKILLS IN THIS CHAPTER

- Leading practices in presentation skills and building effective presentation materials
- How to win over an audience quickly
- Ending a presentation effectively and other suggestions to implement immediately to improve presentations
- Reading body language

KEY WORDS

- Presentations
- Public Speaking
- Body Movement

- Voice Inflection
- Confidence

The statistics on fear of public speaking are vastly exaggerated, but glossophobia is very real. Glossophobia, the formal name for public speaking fear, occurs when a person is performing or about to perform a speech or give a presentation in front of other people.[1] Approximately a quarter of adults report experiencing it.[2] Dalton always felt very natural in front of an audience, even though he never took a course or read a book on it. He was once like every other corporate America employee: graduate from college, go to work for a large company, progress, make money, retire. But something life-changing happened along the way.

Preparing for this course with a long morning workout, Dalton reminisced about key moments in his professional evolution. Twelve years ago, he was a vice president at Sham Pop, a popular drink company that is part of a much larger portfolio. SP, as everyone called it, had grown into a Fortune 500 company. Dalton enjoyed his role there but knew that his upward mobility was now limited. He did not see eye to eye with the senior vice president, Bella Ramirez. There were many issues with Bella and those issues were not readily resolved, particularly because there was a minimal age difference between the two: it can be difficult managing people with similar experience as you. Bella was intelligent but she only cared about one person—herself. Her leadership skills were underdeveloped and she seemed not to trust anyone. This distrust lead Bella to accuse Dalton of trying to take her job and to undermine his attempts to transfer to other areas.

Dalton was working from home one Wednesday morning and went to grab coffee. While waiting on his venti light mocha with an extra shot of espresso, he looked around the coffee shop and was genuinely confused at what he saw. How, on a fall Wednesday morning, were there so many adults just hanging out? Why weren't these people at work?

Dalton was raised with a much different mentality. His father had worked at the same company for 43 years prior to his retirement. His three brothers (one older, two younger) all worked at large companies like Dalton. All

---

[1] "Why Are We Scared of Public Speaking? *Psychology Today,* November 27, 2017 (https://www.psychologytoday.com/us/blog/smashing-the-brainblocks/201711/why-are-we-scared-public-speaking)
[2] Ibid.

were relatively successful. Dalton assumed most of the customers at the coffee shop were either (a) writers, possibly successful but mostly failing, or (b) independently wealthy. Whatever it was, Dalton wanted to understand it and was extremely envious of this lifestyle.

Fast forward a few months and his relationship with Bella continued to deteriorate. His work product was impeccable but things with Bella were not going to get better. This was impacting his personal life greatly. When he was home, he was not mentally home. He stopped talking to his wife. His only outlets were working out and drinking too much. Then, something magical happened. He found himself very distant at Caleb's birthday party at Chuck E. Cheese. His wife noticed. His mom noticed. Everyone noticed. Even the guest who was most checked out with his kids and overfocused on his career noticed.

Dalton's father pulled him aside and told him, "Son, if you are this miserable or overwhelmed by work, ask yourself, is it worth it? I spent 43 years dedicated to a job that, looking back, provided us sustenance and nothing more. I passed up many opportunities for consistency. This company used and abused me. Did they provide a decent living and good retirement? Yes. Did they destroy my relationship with your mom and never give me a chance to have a true relationship with my boys? Yes. You are smart. You work harder than anyone else. If you are not happy, quit. You have money and we can help you. You will figure it out, but don't make the same mistakes I did."

For his own father, with whom he did not have any kind of real relationship with, to recognize this and give him advice, was shocking, to say the least. On Monday, he went in and told Bella it was time for a change. It was the scariest and most freeing period of his life.

After 60 minutes on the elliptical machine, Dalton took to the weights. He thought back on what took him the route of public speaking and executive coaching. Throughout his life, Dalton always wanted to be a writer. He wrote for some basketball websites in his 20s, trying to convert his love of the game into a career. At Sham Pop, Dalton published a few articles that were very well regarded in trade magazines. He still had that first article framed in his office. After the article was published, he had a few incoming calls to come speak at industry association meetings. He figured it would not hurt to give it a try.

After finishing up with dumbbell curls, he casually smiled at himself in the mirror. He recalled the stress of getting up in front of a lunch group of 50 in Fort Worth. He was dressed immaculately: suit pants, vest, French-cuffed shirt, double-Windsor knotted tie, and coordinating pocket square. He was exuding confidence—a very false, contrived confidence. He had many people offering unsolicited advice:

> "If you are using PowerPoint, you need a slide for every two minutes of speaking."
>
> "Don't solicit feedback from the audience; bring your notes and stay on topic and on task throughout."
>
> "Don't field questions until the end; it will throw you off."
>
> "If you get nervous, stand behind the podium."
>
> "Bring notes and look at them as necessary throughout."
>
> "You don't need notes if your slides have a lot of information in them."

Very similar to the unsolicited advice Dalton and his wife received when they first had kids, from friends who did not have kids, it was relatively useless.

Dalton's first presentation was challenging. He tried to be humorous (at least he thought his jokes were funny) to no avail. He attempted to engage the audience throughout and was met with blank stares. He was supposed to present for 60 minutes, but the entire session ran a whole 38 minutes, with no questions at the end whatsoever! On the trip home, he called his wife and told her that he never wanted to do this again. On the other hand, after an experience like that, it could not get much worse. In fact, it got much better, which has led Dalton down a path that he could not be more excited about.

After leaving Sham Pop, he did not know what he wanted to do. The positions he applied for were not interesting or exciting to him. He had a young family, so he could only not work for so long. Over the previous few years, he had been a guest speaker 10 to 15 times a year at different events and received very good feedback. He thought about starting his own training and coaching firm and put out some initial feelers. Those initial feelers proved somewhat fruitful, and then an old friend from Arthur Andersen (Brad Lester) reconnected and needed training, coaching, and co-sourcing. Everything took off from there. Dalton had been very blessed with a lifestyle of his choice and loved sharing what he had learned with everyone.

It had been a few weeks since he had seen Kelli and worked through the Julianne issue. He was excited to be back. The people he met had left a strong impression on him. Good, hard-working people, doing their best to be successful. He knew the team he was working with today desperately needed his assistance. Kelli's team consisted of five department heads who were technically savvy but lacking some personality and leadership. The team consisted of:

- Angela Barnes, Human Resources
- Austin Richards, Information Technology
- Jeffrey Tiller, Budgeting and Forecasting
- Lauren Snow, Accounting/SEC Reporting
- Rodger Smith, Internal Audit

The goal today was to discuss leading practices in public speaking and the challenges the team was facing. Then he planned on recording each and critically evaluating their presentations. Dalton loved this class. There was nothing more eye-opening and unnerving than seeing yourself on video. To this day, Dalton still cringed seeing himself on video, even though he had logged thousands of hours in front of audiences.

The morning began with a group discussion about their major concerns. The team was very well respected inside the organization from a technical standpoint. They were all very polished and presented well, but they appeared a bit stiff and unassuming. Kelli wanted to do this with her team because they were all relatively inexperienced and wanted to improve themselves prior to the significant growth the company was forecasted to have.

Angela was dressed in a navy blue business suit with matching heels. Her appearance was very striking: tall, athletic, long blonde hair, and deep-sea-blue eyes. Austin might be the physical opposite of Angela. Approximately five feet nine inches tall, he had a broad stature, and dark red hair and a thick full beard that covered his neck. Being in IT, Austin was more casually dressed, in khaki pants and a forest green sweater. Jeffrey Tiller looked the part of an accountant: tall, skinny, with black short hair neatly parted to the left, Jeffrey (not Jeff) wore brown pants, a short-sleeve button-up yellow shirt, and thick glasses.

Lauren was about five foot seven, athletic, with a dark complexion, jet black hair, dark brown almond eyes, and black-rimmed glasses. She was very professionally dressed in a black pant suit and white blouse. Finally, Rodger was well dressed, in black pants and gray blazer; he had a dark complexion and brown eyes. He also sported Dalton's favorite hairstyle: a shaved head. Because Dalton enjoyed self-deprecating humor, he liked to say that everyone knows it is a style choice and not a necessity.

The team shared their biggest concerns, which were diverse but very similar in nature:

- Angela felt very confident speaking to her team one-on-one or in small groups. When in front of a large audience, she was intimidated by having a large group stare at her. It made her very nervous and caused her to forget and stutter.

- Austin is an introvert at heart and does not mind speaking with peers because he can use technical jargon and speak at a level he is comfortable with. When he goes outside of IT, he struggles to connect with anyone.
- Jeffrey is similar to Austin: great at accounting, can talk the talk, but struggles to connect with people who cannot speak his language.
- Lauren was the most refined of the team and seemed very confident in front of peers. She was hoping to pick up some tips and continue to improve her group presentation skills. She was young, so Dalton was impressed with her confidence and taken aback by her cockiness.
- Rodger appeared professional and well-spoken. Dalton struggled to find an issue with how he would present in front of a group because he came off very polished. After an hour of observing the group interact, he pegged Rodger's issue: he sometimes came across as very condescending, speaking down to people and using words that are not common. This could be due to his Ivy League education. Rodger did not realize that he was very similar to Austin: neither could connect with groups, but for very different reasons.

Dalton spent the morning leading the discussion and developing rapport with the team. He had met many of them a few weeks back when he was investigating the Julianne issue but did not have a chance to speak to any of them in depth. Julianne, in fact, did not come up throughout the day. He needed to check with Kelli on what they were planning on doing.

Dalton would personalize his interactions and look for common themes to bond over. He was not sure of each of team's personal status, so he spoke about himself to humanize himself. He spoke glowingly of Caleb and Liora and how he is an avid reader, sports fan, and yogi. Angela was separated but has a daughter similar in age to Liora. Austin is a fanatical Golden State Warriors fan and he and Dalton bonded over their mutual love of basketball. Dalton, from Dallas, is a long-time Mavericks season ticket holder, and they discussed the Mavericks–Warriors series from 2007, one of the biggest upsets in basketball history, as the eighth-seeded Warriors beat the top-seeded Mavericks in six games. This memory still stuck in Dalton's craw.

Dalton was able to speak accounting with Jeffrey, which made him much more comfortable. Lauren was easy to talk to; she seemed interested in anything and everything Dalton had to say. She was also very easy to get lost in. Dalton was also a master of making the person he was talking to feel like they were the only other person in the room.

Dalton struggled with Rodger; he tended to struggle with academics. Dalton was very well educated (two degrees from Texas A&M University) but he had learned many years ago to speak at a level that everyone can connect with. In fact, he learned this being around Caleb and Liora when they were young. He would use words they didn't understand and they'd react with the classic inquisitive child questions: "Why?" or "What does that mean?" or "Huh?" He knew he had to speak in plain English to connect with them, or to really connect with anyone.

As Dalton knew, there are five language registers or styles. Each level has an appropriate use that is determined by varying situations—the audience (who), the topic (what), the purpose (why), and location (where). The five language registers are:

1. **Static Register:** This style *rarely* changes. It is "frozen" in time and content (e.g. the Pledge of Allegiance, laws).
2. **Formal Register:** Used in formal settings, this style is one-way communication. Such use of language usually follows a commonly accepted format, impersonal and formal. This is common for speeches (e.g. sermons, speeches, and announcements).
3. **Consultative Register:** This is the standard form where people engage in a mutually accepted structure of communication. It is formal/professional and in line with societal expectations (e.g. between strangers, between an employee and supervisor, between doctor and patient).
4. **Casual Register:** This is informal language used by peers and friends. Slang, vulgarities, and colloquialisms are normal. This is "group" language and could also include texting.
5. **Intimate Register:** This communication is private, reserved for close family members or intimate people (e.g. spouse, significant other, siblings, parents and children).[3]

Dalton thought that Rodger stuck to formal in most cases, a mistake many speakers make. People can usually transition from one language register to an adjacent one without encountering any major issues, but skipping one or more levels is confusing, to say the least. Dalton did believe that moving down the scale was prudent. He might start at Formal, quickly ease into Consultative

---

[3] Montano-Harmon, M.R. "Developing English for Academic Purposes," California State University, Fullerton.

and, by the end of the presentation, depending on the audience, nature, and format of the presentation, he would switch to Casual or potentially Intimate. He always wanted to personalize the experience as much as possible.

The rest of the day progressed well. Kelli popped in periodically to check on the team and sit in for a few minutes at a time before running to another meeting. Dalton asked her not to stay so the team would feel free to speak openly and hold nothing back. He certainly received that and more. Angela bared her soul, discussing deep-seated issues about being in front of groups, originating in her youth. She was on the verge of crying a few times. Some might think that was "too much" but Dalton found her attitude and honesty refreshing. To be able to speak so candidly and be vulnerable in front of other senior leaders was impressive. She was definitely using this session as therapeutic relief. Dalton, being observant, picked up on the attentiveness of Austin, Rodger, and Jeffrey while Angela was speaking. They seemed very interested and respectful of her emotions. He also picked up on Lauren's subtle eye rolls when Angela spoke. When the rest of the team spoke, Lauren displayed the body language of someone very interested in the topic at hand:

- Upright posture or leaning in toward the person speaking when she was focusing or when she was very interested in what was being said
- Legs and body facing the person speaking
- Hands (when leaning forward) on the table directly in front of her, connected or taking notes
- Legs crossed but minimal movement
- Head turning slightly when considering what was being said

Yet when Angela spoke, Lauren's demeanor changed strikingly and her body language revealed this drastic change:

- Leaning back in her chair
- Arms crossed or hands connected behind her head
- Leg beginning to twitch when crossed
- Would not make eye contact with Angela
- Frequent eye rolls
- Low sound effects (blowing air, sighing, etc.)

There was definitely something there that Dalton needed to understand further. He firmly believed that Angela was sincere. He did not have a baseline to compare to her current demeanor but there were telltale signs of someone

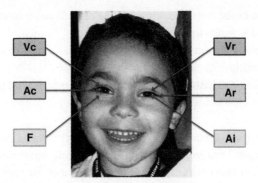

FIGURE 7.1 Neurolinguistic programming: eye cues.

being honest. When Angela spoke, she tended to show her palms, which is an indicator of sincerity. Palms down could be viewed as the person has something to hide. When recalling the root cause of her fear, she would look to her left and pause. Dalton could imagine the cartoon bubble right next to her, filled with the exact moment she was remembering. Dalton also observed that Angela was right-handed. When recalling a moment, right-handed people tend to look to their left. When constructing, righties tend to look to their right. (The opposite would be true for people that are predominantly left-handed.) At this moment, he pictured one of his favorite slides and topics from his courses: neurolinguistic programming, specifically to a person's eye cues (Figure 7.1). He loved this slide because he used a picture of his son as a young child to talk about this topic. Such a cute picture of such a sweet boy, but a sweet boy who could sure spin a tale or two. When he discussed this topic, he spoke specifically of Caleb, because Dalton believed that you could read a child's eyes better than an adult's. To an extent, adults learned how to mask some of these "tells," but kids did not know better. Dalton specifically observed Caleb's eyes when he was determining if he was telling the truth.

In general, a person's eyes tend to look in a specific direction when recalling information (to their left) or constructing information (to their right). (This assumes our subject is right-handed; the opposite would be true for someone who is predominantly left-handed.) The six quadrants are as follows:

- **Visually Constructed:** Constructing a site mentally (making up a story)
- **Visually Remembered:** Remembering something that has occurred (seen)
- **Audio Constructed:** Creating a sound or imagining what something sounds like

- **Audio Remembered:** Recalling what a certain voice (sounds like or any other sound) sounds like
- **Feeling/Kinesthetic:** Remembering how something smelled, or tasted, or a specific feeling
- **Auditory Digital/Internal Dialog:** When someone might talk to themselves; some type of internal dialog[4]

Dalton knew these should be used tactfully; the entire package must be accounted for: body language, facial expressions, tone, voice inflection, and eye cues. He also knew there was much hidden information in a person's eyes. And he knew his eyes moved to neurolinguistic programming like one of his favorite songs. In fact, he had to watch himself because he would look down to the right quite often. Traveling alone, the person he most spoke to was himself!

Austin, being an introvert, was quiet but observant throughout the afternoon. Dalton made sure to bring him into most conversations, especially the ones he showed interest in (without saying anything). Jeffrey was similar but seemed more comfortable talking among his peers. He spoke regularly and made some poignant observations. Rodger was interested and engaged but, again, seemed above some of the conversations.

Dalton wrapped up the afternoon with the team preparing their presentations for the next the morning. Dalton asked each to prepare a short presentation (less than fifteen minutes) on their department and key performance indicators over the prior period. What he did not tell the team was that he had asked Kelli to have 20 to 30 employees from their teams attend each presentation, including planting questions and distractions. This was a very intelligent, well-spoken team. Dalton wanted to challenge them.

Prior to leaving for the day, Dalton debriefed with Kelli about the inner workings of the team. When he mentioned what he observed from Lauren, Kelli (ironically) let out a sigh, not-so-subtly rolled her eyes, and filled Dalton in.

"Lauren is great. She has endless potential. To be 31 and as advanced as she is truly remarkable. She has earned every promotion she has received. She does come off immature at times, specifically with Angela. I do not think she trusts Angela at all. But I do not think there is any history there. Angela wears her emotions on her sleeve and Lauren is very much the opposite. I think Lauren believes Angela utilizes emotion to manipulate people. Lauren wants to be judged on her merits. Nothing more. Nothing less." Dalton thought he could assist with this.

---

[4] https://www.nlpworld.co.uk/nlp-glossary/e/eye-accessing-cues/

After wrapping up with Kelli, Dalton walked over to the downtown Hilton, changed quickly, and went down to the gym for a quick session on the elliptical and weightlifting. Dinner with Kelli and her family would be tomorrow night. He had been putting in double time on the road as much as possible and could feel the road starting to take its toll. He had gained some weight and wanted to make sure it stayed at that or dropped a bit. Dalton used this time to plan the rest of his week: what he accomplished today, what needed to be done for the rest of the week, and longer-term plans. He would also spend this time zoned-out and daydreaming, thinking about Caleb scoring a big goal, Liora doing her thing academically, his own first book coming out, or something of the like. It helped him push through those moments when he definitely needed the extra kick.

Most days, he loved his alone time and needed it after speaking to people all day. He rarely went out for dinner on the road, but tonight the thought of being alone in his room would drive him crazy. He took a quick shower, threw on his Adidas Firebird tracksuit and running shoes, grabbed his computer bag, and went down the street to Quakes Sports Bar, owned by one of the former NASL players for the San Jose Earthquakes. When in town, Dalton always stopped in because he was an avid soccer fan and collected sports memorabilia from defunct sports leagues.

Dalton found a quiet corner, ordered his Absolut and soda and a blackened salmon Caesar salad, opened his MacBook Air, and sorted through his emails. His waitress, Dahlia, dropped off his drink. (Dalton was obsessed with learning and remembering people's names.) He was knee-deep in his emails when he finally peered up from the laptop screen to check out the score in the Warriors game. In the distance, out of the corner of his eye, he saw someone who looked like Lauren. She still wore her black-rimmed glasses but had changed into a much more casual outfit: a short navy blue sweater, jeans, and brown ankle boots. Her long black hair was pulled back into a casual ponytail. She was sitting with an attractive young man who appeared to be younger than she was. The gentleman wore slacks, a dress shirt, and sport coat.

Dalton loved to people-watch. In fact, he could say this was research. The past 10 years, he had been steeped in research. His undergrad degree was in accounting and he had obtained his master's in finance. When he worked in corporate America, he used his technical skills wrapped up with his soft skills. Once he went into coaching and training, he began to use his soft skills more and more. People-watching was his training ground.

Lauren exhibited similar body language to earlier in the day: disinterested in the conversation, nodding her head often but without intent. This seemed to be more of a distraction tactic, to make it look like she was listening, but even a casual observer would pick up on her disinterest. Her crossed leg was moving very fast. She drank her clear cocktail fast, appearing to attempt to numb herself to the conversation. Her facial expressions showed boredom and a general lack of interest. She avoided eye contact and had minimal facial expression, except for the casual fake smile and laugh.

Dalton found her dismissiveness comical, especially after chatting with Kelli. He knew she was very personable but tended to turn it on and off as necessary. She had not seen him, so when Dahlia came by to check on him, he asked her to bring Lauren another drink—she looked like she needed it. He did tell Dahlia not to mention who it came from; he thought she would be able to figure it out relatively quickly.

Another 45 minutes went by. Dalton returned to his emails and planning and, with his headphone volume up, zoned out from the world. He quietly ate and surfed through LinkedIn for no real reason. He picked up his third drink and sipped it through the stirring straw (an annoying habit he picked up many years ago that he could not break), when he looked up to see Lauren with a very different look—a beautiful, cheek-to-cheek smile. She asked to sit down and they chatted for a while. In fact, they chatted for much more than a while. Time seemed to fly by as they got to know each other. She discussed her blind date; she thought he was really cute but Xavier was an investment broker and three years younger than her, and it showed. He came off somewhat immature and she was taken aback by his lingo; he spoke as he would text. She became bored quickly.

"I go out with younger guys on occasion, just to see if I could date someone younger, and then dates like this remind me that I have no interest in that potential immaturity. They are nice to look at—but then they speak!" Lauren said with a semi-sarcastic laugh. She was speaking pretty rudely but even Dalton let out a hearty laugh because he felt the same.

At 44, dating for Dalton was challenging, not necessarily due to his age, but to his schedule and priorities. His priorities, he believed, were in line with anyone with a family and a growing business:

1. Family
2. Religion
3. Work
4. Family
5. Working Out
6. Work
7. Personal Life

When he first separated from his wife, he dated quite a bit. He thought that was what you were supposed to do. Many women he had met over the years seemed interested regardless of his marital status. He made sure not to burn any bridges with potential clients and had the opportunity to date many amazing women. The problem was his priorities. He was rarely home and when he was, it was family time, Caleb's soccer, and other similar commitments. He dated more often out of town. That also brought up the obvious problem of not being there enough. He dated a few friends for the past few years but it teetered between dating and friendship every time they saw each other. Both he and his female friends loved being together, but it was a significant letdown the weeks after they spent time together.

Lauren was 31 but she was mature beyond her years. She struggled to find a good match. Dalton thought that this seemed predictable. He was a very good read of people and someone as intelligent and driven as Lauren would intimidate men, regardless of age. She definitely enjoyed dating older men but that was challenging. Many of the "good guys" were married or came with plenty of baggage. After a while, Dalton—being the type of person who can ask anybody anything—blurted out that he knew what type of guys she dated and what type of guys she should date. Lauren, intrigued by what she was hearing, with a flirty smile and a sip of her drink, asked him to continue.

"You date guys your friends say you are supposed to date. You are young and successful so you date young and successful. You date men younger than you, potentially many years younger. The problem is that many men are intimidated by you. So, you go out on dates with guys who will never fit long-term." He paused for impact. "Maybe that is really what you are ready for, so maybe you purposely date guys who won't fit."

You could immediately tell that she was truly considering what Dalton said. Everything he said was either correct or mostly correct. She was pondering the last statement. Dalton picked up on this when her head turned partially to the side, her right eye squinting and her eyebrows slightly furrowed. While he was speaking she leaned forward in her chair, but then pulled back and paused for consideration.

Dalton had to watch himself. He did not want Lauren to think he was flirting with her. Although he found her very attractive both in person and, more importantly, mentally, he did not want to cross any boundaries. He had too much respect for Kelli to even consider that.

After taking a few more sips of her drink, she smiled and asked Dalton, "So, what is your situation? You are so good at reading me. Tell me about you." Dalton laughed as Lauren casually changed the subject. He smiled and did not bother commenting; based on her reaction, he was very confident that he had hit a chord. Dalton answered the question and they continued to chat until well after midnight. Dalton walked Lauren to her Uber, gave her a hug and a kiss on the cheek, and hustled back to the hotel. Lauren hugged back very warmly and held on for an extra second. Dalton appreciated her warmth.

The next morning, Dalton got in early to set up the room and had his "plants"—the people who would run off a script and challenge the speakers—prepared well before anyone else was in the office. On days like this, Dalton loved his job even more. He loved to challenge people, to take them out of their comfort zone, and for many of the team this would be taking them out of their comfort zones.

Dalton thought about letting the team pick the order of speaking, but after yesterday's dialogue, he thought it would be prudent to go ahead and set the order himself:

1. Jeffrey Tiller
2. Lauren Snow
3. Angela Barnes
4. Austin Richards
5. Rodger Smith

Jeffrey and Lauren seemed comfortable speaking in front of groups, so he wanted to get the rest of the team warmed up and more comfortable in front of the group. The contrarian view was that Angela and Austin would have a high standard to meet going next but Dalton thought it was a worthwhile risk. Angela and Austin will be the most nervous, and Rodger—well, Dalton wasn't certain if he cared enough to put in the effort so it was an easy decision to have him bring up the rear. Dalton made sure his videographer, Mike, was also set and ready to go. It was important that everyone was thinking through how to optimize a presentation.

Preparation for any presentation begins with identifying your audience:

- Who is the audience?
- What do you know about them?
- Do they care about the topic?
- Should they care about the topic?
- What's important to them?
- Do they have any misconceptions about your topic?
- Could there be a lack of understanding?
- Can you predict the questions they might have?

Dalton strongly believed that going through this while preparing a presentation was definitely necessary, especially for novice presenters, because it helps give a basic structure for the speech, which the presenter can add to and take away from as necessary. Dalton created an audience profile/questionnaire for all clients to use:

- **Education:** Regardless of education and savviness, speak to the same level you are taught to write to (middle school). If the audience is well-versed in the technical language of the topic, that can definitely be used without a detailed explanation.
- **Familiarity with Topic:** What do people know about the topic already and what do you need to explain? Is this a controversial topic?
- **Audience:** Who in the audience do we need to get on our side? Who is the pulse-setter of the group? Is this presentation to convince the group of something, or to mediate an issue between groups?
- **Interest in the Topic:** Do they care about the topic? What do people care about? Is this topic important to them? What's important to them?
- **Possible Misconceptions:** Which incorrect ideas might you need to correct? In most cases, this should be addressed at the beginning of the presentation. Until this is addressed, the audience will be confused and their guard will be up.
- **Attitude:** Are people hostile, supportive, curious, worried? The attitude of your audience will affect the tone of your speech. The time of day and day of week will also potentially impact the attitude.

Dalton knew this would be a topic of conversation because the team did not have insight into the audience. Quite frankly, they did not know there would be an audience! Dalton taught the team that gaining and keeping the attention of an audience and speaking to what interests them is the most important thing about any speech. It is not about what you say, but how you say it. Consider the best way to deliver a message and consider how that message will be communicated best to the audience you are addressing. One of the quotes attributed to Dalton that he said at the beginning of his career trended on LinkedIn for a while:

> The goal of communication is not merely to communicate a message. The goal of communication is to gain acceptance and understanding of the message.

He knew this was the most common mistake for novice presenters. They want to get the presentation over with and are not as concerned with how, what, and why—just get it delivered. He thought he might see that with Angela, Austin, or potentially Rodger.

Everyone was set up as the team came in. Lauren was first to arrive, wearing tan high heels, a navy mid-length skirt, white button-up shirt, and navy jacket. She looked striking and professional. She carried a venti coffee, as well as what appeared to be a large iced coffee (with cream and Sweet 'N Low). Their drink of choice had come up during their conversation the previous night and she was nice enough to bring it for Dalton. Truly a sweet gesture.

Angela walked in right after and Dalton did a double take. She owned the room as soon as she entered. She was dressed in a red skirt, tight black knee-high boots, and a white tight-fitting sweater. Her hair was straightened and her hands were freshly manicured. She was definitely dressed to impress. Jeffrey, Austin, and Rodger walked in together and were bantering about the Warriors game of the night before. The team had seen a precipitous fall this season due to injuries to Curry and Thompson and free agent losses.

Everybody was ready to go, so Dalton invited Jeffrey to start. Dalton had asked each team member to speak for 15 minutes or less on their department: mission statement, key objectives, strategic initiatives, and the biggest challenges over the coming year. Dalton chose this because of its relevance to the audience and the speaker; it was a topic all should find easy to embrace. The team was caught off guard by the audience in attendance but seemed to adjust quickly.

To his credit, Jeffrey started out with some humor to warm up the audience. He mentioned some of last year's accomplishments and stated, "We do not plan to be this year's Warriors; we plan on following up last year's strong performance with more of the same!" The audience enjoyed the humor and it relaxed any tension that existed. Jeffrey went through the presentation smoothly. The mood and opinion of any audience is important. It will influence the tone and content of the speech; a nervous or concerned audience will require an element of comfort or reassurance, while an excited audience will want to share a positive, electric atmosphere. This is what Jeffrey did to the group. He was able to get them excited through his positivity and passion. He highlighted last year's accomplishments, called out key team members who made large contributions to the overall success of the team, and followed up with key initiatives for this coming year.

Jeffrey went over the 15-minute allotment, and did not field many questions at all. Dalton wrote a note to himself to discuss this with Jeffrey since he considered this is important. Speakers will lose their audience quickly if they go over their time allotment. This is something Dalton always strived for:

always end early. People tend to get impatient when running up against a time deadline. Everyone can relate to attending a training session where the speaker went over the time allotment. Regardless of how fun and interesting the topic is, once you hit your deadline, the time creeps by; one minute feels like ten minutes, or even more.

Dalton also felt strongly that a speaker should engage the audience throughout the presentation. Unless the presentation is designed to be controlling (such as a town hall meeting), engaging an audience will make everyone pay attention more intently. Hearing one voice consistently for a period of time is more challenging to pay attention to than hearing numerous voices and banter over the same period of time and on the same topic. Dalton always contended that speakers who hold questions till the end were not good presenters; it meant they did not want to be interrupted and most likely indicated that they were presenting through memory. Had they memorized their presentation, it would not feel fluid, with a good chance it would be monotone. Jeffrey did a very good job but Dalton thought this feedback would be very helpful.

One of the audience members raised their hand at the end of the applause from the group and asked Jeffrey a question. This had been plotted by Dalton. Jon Stanley, one of the managers on the team, asked Jeffrey about upgrading the current forecasting software and the potential to add staff the next year. Dalton knew these were contentious issues for Jeffrey and, based on Jeffrey's body language, he was definitely caught offguard by this. Jon attempted to hold it together and not smile, because Jeffrey knew it was not Jon's nature to ask questions like this during a presentation. Jeffrey caught on quickly but his initial reaction showed he was surprised and definitely did not appreciate being called out.

Dalton had asked Mike to zoom in on the speaker when the planted questions were asked and was excited that Jeffrey would be able to see this replay via video later in the day. Dalton caught Jeffrey exhibiting the following characteristics:

- Eyebrows initially raised, showing surprise
- Head moving backward as the question was asked, literally taken aback by the question
- Eyebrows beginning to furrow as his head moved forward
- Nostrils flared before answering the question
- Arms at his side before the question was asked, slowly moved in front of him and crossed when the question was asked and as he began to answer
- Hand gestures while answering the question; pointing at Jon while speaking (Dalton believed the pointing was unintended.)

Jeffrey regained his composure and answered the question tactfully and directly. Dalton was impressed at his recovery. They took a five-minute break and Jeffrey approached Jon immediately, not in an aggressive manner but with a smile on his face. Dalton ran to the men's room and saw Kelli approaching. She checked in to see how things were going but purposefully was absent from the presentations so as not to add additional stress to the team.

As Dalton reentered the conference room, he felt a hand on his forearm. Lauren came close to him and, with a large grin on her face, whispered how impressed she was with the setup. She told him he had better have something good planned for her, then winked and walked off. Dalton had to continue to watch himself as her flirtatious nature became more obvious.

Lauren walked up confidently and started out with a simple but important gesture: a smile. She had a beautiful smile. Regardless, any smile showed that the speaker was friendly and approachable. She started out with a strong introductory statement:

> As a team, we met all of our financial reporting deadlines but, significantly, we cut 20% off of our reporting calendar this year. We continue to become more efficient every year but, more importantly, our team, led by Annie and David, continue to be as effective as possible. I could not be more thrilled to be a part of such a cohesive and high-performing team.

This garnered a rousing applause from her team. She then asked if there were any comments from the team and Annie and David both chimed in. Dalton continued to take copious notes, jotting down a couple of key points he saw from Lauren:

- When she wanted to emphasize a point, she edged away from the podium and closer to the group of 40. She moved right in front of them and used both hands to emphasize her affection for the team.
- She also stated that she was "part of the team" versus "leading the team" or calling them "my team." This was subtle but important. Lauren knew her personal success was dependent on her team, so she always tried to speak in terms of "ours" versus "mine."
- She altered her voice inflection throughout the initial monologue. She spoke with conviction and passion when talking about last year's accomplishments. And she spoke with concern but confidence when speaking of this year's challenges.

Lauren wrapped up in eight minutes, including some dialogue and questions from the team. She offered to field some questions after her wrap-up slide but there were none. Dalton loved this ending but planned to suggest one tweak to really take her presentations to the next level. He wholeheartedly subscribed to the theory that if your message as a presenter is readily accepted and you foster an interactive environment, there will be few if any questions at the end. He planned on discussing with Lauren and the team in the afternoon.

Dalton always struggled to understand why presenters ended with a Q and A session. As a presenter, you want your message to be flexible but you also want to control the message. A simple sales messaging tactic is to introduce your message, reiterate/support your message, and conclude with your ask or key message. If you end with Q and A, you might lose control of your message. There is a strong possibility that your conclusion is not as strong or is forgotten through the potentially irrelevant questions or questions that the presenter cannot answer.

When Dalton first started in this business, this was something he changed immediately. Prior to his final slide or final message, Dalton would always pause and ask for any final questions or comments. Similar to Lauren's method, there was rarely more than one question. Quite frequently, all had been answered and he would roll into his final concluding slide. On this slide, he would summarize the three key messages he wanted everyone leaving the room with. He subscribed to the rule of three: three is the lowest number that can form a pattern in our minds.[5] People remember messages when they are simplified and easy to digest. Studies have shown that human recall is much better when the message is grouped in threes. So Dalton focused on this in his summary slide and made sure that slide had the three most relevant messages he wanted the audience to leave with. He honestly did not understand why presenters ended with a Q and A. He had concluded that many novice presenters either did not know any better; this was how they were taught and what they had previously experienced. When we do not know that there is another way, we fall into these vicious cycles. Dalton made it a point to reiterate this message in all his classes and this got to be his signature; he became known for this messaging.

Everyone adjourned after Lauren's presentation. Lauren had performed admirably and she walked out of the room with high confidence. Dalton waited for her outside the conference room to have a short sidebar. She strutted quickly out of the room and walked past Dalton without seeing him. He

---

[5] https://school.iqdoodle.com/framework/core-principles/rule-of-three/

grabbed her arm and she came to an abrupt stop, seeing Dalton, smiling, and appearing very happy to hear his feedback. He was professional and did not give her the full attention she craved. He mentioned that he was impressed and she did a good job. Dalton noticed by her facial expressions that she was disappointed with the lack of elaboration. She showed this by:

- Smile slowly changing to a neutral expression
- Eyebrows raised, moving back to resting position
- Letting go of his forearm and moving back subtly

Dalton did not want her to get the impression that he did not enjoy the presentation or her company. He leaned in close and whispered, "You did a fantastic job. I definitely have some pointers and have some ideas I want to run by you but you have *it* and not many people have *it*." Lauren smiled openly, blushing brightly for everyone to see, and thanked him. She then leaned in and told him she knew of better places to go than Quakes and if he was free, she would love to take him. Her excitement turned to slight disappointment as he mentioned he had plans with Kelli and her family. He did state that he was leaving early to see Kelli's kids and he could grab a bite or at least a drink later that evening. The roller coaster of emotions Lauren was showing turned to contentment as she heard this and was excited about what the evening would bring.

Angela prepared to start and the room could sense her nervousness. It still surprised Dalton that someone who presented herself so well could be so nervous. Her voice slowly fluttered due to her nerves. In order to focus, she hid herself behind the podium. Dalton always said this was the indication of someone who was physically hiding. This was like a safety blanket, or like home base when playing tag; no one could touch you when you were there. Angela stood behind the podium for the first few minutes, reading from her slides in a very nervous voice and no change in tone or voice inflection. She turned her back to her audience to read, which was another no-no.

Dalton readily turned his back to his audience as he would constantly move around through his presentation. This was purposeful, to engage the audience because they would have to reposition themselves to see him and his voice would be heard from many different directions. Dalton also determined his constant movement served his need to get to 15,000 steps a day and calmed his then-undiagnosed ADHD. When Dalton turned his back, he was usually behind the group and facing them. In essence, he had not turned around. He would, on occasion, turn his back when in front of a group but this was to quickly gather the contents of a slide, read them, and comment. He did not read each slide; in fact, he made sure his slides did not contain complete sentences or thoughts. The slides did not stand alone; they were there to jog his memory on where to go with this initial statement.

Dalton knew Angela was struggling. He liked everyone on the team but he took a special liking to Angela. He saw her potential and that he had the ability to really help her change. Instead of taking notes, Dalton got up from his chair and quickly walked to the middle of the back of the room (he was seated in the back near the door). Angela's eyes caught Dalton walking. Seeing this, Dalton gestured for her to move from behind the podium and mouthed, "Move around." Since he had Angela's attention, he moved his hands to in front of his face and widened them to outside of his cheeks, gesturing her to smile. This made her smile unconsciously. She paused, walked from behind the podium that was in front of the room, and moved to the center of the room to continue. Her presentation pace picked up. This showed she was still nervous. After a minute, she looked back at Dalton, who gestured for her to breathe by taking his hands at his chest and motioning them up to his face as he took a deep breath and moving them back down to the position they started as he exhaled. Angela took the cue and took a breath and paused. She smiled again, and this seemed to help her relax. The remainder of her presentation improved greatly.

Austin seemed to learn from Angela's slow start. Prior to Austin's presentation, Dalton had advised him to be himself. "If you try to be someone else, people will sense it. You are an introvert; that does not mean you have to be introverted all the time but the most important thing is to be yourself. Regardless of how outgoing you are, be yourself. People will appreciate the authenticity of you being you." Austin took this to heart and presented slowly but surely. He calmly went through the presentation without much voice inflection, but it was still effective.

Since Austin oversaw one of the most important and controversial departments, Dalton had planted a few questions from attendees. Since Austin presented fourth, he knew this was coming and handled the contentious questions pretty well.

Dalton was greatly anticipating Rodger's turn because he really had no idea what he was going to see. Would Rodger be prepared and engaged, or generally dismissive? Dalton leaned to the former because Rodger was a professional. Dalton was very interested to see the engagement he would get from his team. He had no doubt that Rodger was respected but was concerned about whether his team truly liked him and if he could get the best out of them.

Rodger started strong and engaged the group. You could definitely see that some of his employees were disengaged and might lack respect for Rodger.

Rodger tended to speak above people and seemed to enjoy flaunting his intelligence. Dalton was also concerned how Rodger appeared to other leaders in the organization. As the head of internal audit, it was critical for Rodger to have good relationships and be respected by other department heads and executive management. If not, the value his department could bring to the organization would be limited.

The presentations wrapped up around 11:00 and they all enjoyed a quick catered lunch. Dalton spent some time with Mike and gave him guidance on how to edit the videos and what specific scenes he wanted to focus on.

He began to debrief after lunch and wanted to solicit everyone's thoughts on each other. He thought peer reviews were a good way to give and receive feedback. It also meant much more to hear it from their peers. The only problem with this approach was that everyone was way too nice. Dalton knew that, in order to preserve relationships, people would not be completely honest. Or at least they thought they were preserving relationships. Dalton had this bitter honesty type of relationship with Brad. Brad was always one to tell him the way it is. Dalton believed that was one of the reasons why they were so close.

Lauren and Jeffrey spoke confidently about their results. Angela brimmed with pride about how she was able to recover from her very bad start. Austin smiled lightly, seemingly always holding in all emotion. Rodger, as always, seemed indifferent. Dalton told everyone the plan: watch the videos and discuss as a team tomorrow afternoon after Mike had a chance to edit and Dalton had a chance to review.

As they left to head back to their offices, Austin stopped to thank Dalton sincerely for his advice. He also asked if he was available tomorrow morning to speak about a different topic altogether. "I spoke to Kelli about an issue I have with one of my team members; I wanted to run it by you and get your thoughts." Dalton planned to meet Austin mid-morning.

In order to prepare his presentation, it would take Dalton three or four hours to analyze the videos and formalize his notes, even after Mike edited and finalized the videos. He had worked with Mike for the last few years and Mike knew exactly what Dalton was looking for in most cases. Dalton went back to the hotel, checked email, and got a quick workout prior to heading over to Kelli's to spend some time with her family.

Kelli and Baxter had been married for almost 10 years. They seemed to have a great relationship—a true-life partnership. Dalton enjoyed spending time with them because they exemplified what he wanted in a partner. Baxter was a writer with a work-from-home consulting business. He was relatively successful but when Kelli's career took off, he took a step back and went the home business route so he could stay home with the kids. The kids (Daniel, age five, and the twins, Banner and Chisholm, age three) were very close to their father, for obvious reasons. Dalton brought the kids Luka Dončić jerseys; the kids were fanatical basketball fans and Dončić played for the Dallas Mavericks and Dalton was slowly converting them to Mavericks fans. Dalton and Baxter were having drinks on the patio and the kids were playing basketball when Kelli got home. The kids were excited to see Mom, but not excited enough to pull them away from their intense game of 21.

Kelli changed and joined the men, catching up on life in general. Dalton was intrigued by Baxter's new book; he had always aspired to write his own book. He thought a book based on a similar premise to his life and travels could have a market. Baxter was planning on assisting him in finding a publisher. Kelli asked about the morning and Dalton filled her in on the highlights. He also mentioned that he was planning on leaving a bit early to have dinner with Lauren. First, he told her how this came about and that she wanted to meet after last night's conversation. Secondly, he told her explicitly that this was professional. Kelli started to laugh and said, "D, why would I care? We are friends; I know you respect me. I hope you can help Lauren, but have fun; I can see you guys getting along very well." Dalton let out a silent sigh of relief. This did not change his plans but he appreciated the confidence and respect she had for him. Dalton said his goodbyes and promised to take the boys to a Mavericks game the next time they were in town.

Dalton grabbed an Uber and met Lauren for dinner around eight at a small hole-in-the-wall Italian restaurant just outside of downtown. Gino's barely had a sign up but the place was bustling with people. Lauren sat in a booth in the back, with a few bottles of wine on the table. Gino's was a bring-your-own-alcohol establishment and it appeared the bar was stocked!

Lauren looked nice in tight jeans, knee-high brown boots, and a loose cream sweater. Her jet-black hair was pulled back in a bun and she had her black-rimmed glasses on. She appeared to be a few glasses of wine ahead of her competition already. Dalton was not sure if he would greet her with a hug or a warm handshake but this was not his decision to make. Lauren made it for him by standing up upon first seeing him and delivering a warm hug, almost jumping into his arms. It was very sweet and Dalton was surprised by her outward affection. Lauren sat on the left side of the booth initially. When she rose to hug Dalton, she moved closer to the center of the booth. Dalton sat down and naturally moved to the center; at this point, there was less than a foot separating the two. Lauren quietly made small talk; she seemed to drink quickly to calm her nerves. Dalton took it as a great compliment that a refined woman like Lauren would be nervous sitting with him.

A large man with a shoulder-length hair and a beard walked over to take their order. The gentleman's hair was much more salt and pepper than black, the sign of advancing age that Dalton was now experiencing full bore. He could tell that Lauren knew this man based on her reaction when he approached the table. She smiled and rolled her eyes; not a condescending eye roll but one she might make to someone who embarrasses her. He smirked internally as this man had to be related to her. The man attempted to keep a straight face and play it as though he did not know Lauren. The man's name was Gino. Dalton said that it was nice to meet him and asked if he was the owner since that was the name of the restaurant. Yes, this was indeed Gino of Gino's Italian.

Dalton ordered a club soda and asked if Lauren was his daughter or niece. Gino smiled (as did Lauren) and they chatted for a bit. Gino was Lauren's uncle and they were very close. Lauren came in weekly but never brought company, except a few close girlfriends. Gino stated that Dalton must be something for her to take him to the restaurant. Everyone laughed and Lauren corrected Gino quickly with a slap to his shoulder and a blushing "Stop!" She evenly stated that she wanted to take him to a restaurant that was truly old San Francisco.

Dalton was honored she "let him in" in that way. Dalton personally did not let many people in. He did not show his true self; he had his public persona that everyone saw. His ex-wife knew him well. His parents and brothers knew him well. Meghan knew Dalton relatively well. Brad knew the true Dalton. Caleb and Liora knew him probably better than anyone. He rarely let anyone else in. Dalton thought how nice it would be to have someone he could confide in, someone he could trust unconditionally.

Dalton was very happy that he had caught a workout prior to going out for the evening because course after course kept coming. Fried cheese, salad, more salad (Dalton, at this point, could not distinguish any of them), numerous pastas, veal, chicken and eggplant parmesan. He wished the kids were with him because they would have enjoyed a feast like this! The food was spectacular: fresh ingredients, cooked to order It truly tasted as if it was cooked with love and affection.

Based on his personality and career, Dalton was truly easy to open up to. Most people would say that they felt comfortable telling him anything, without judgment. This worked very well when investigating potential fraud; people loved to admit things to him. Dalton had always joked that if he was ever single again, he had discovered the key to dating, regardless of physical looks. The audience would always laugh, but once Dalton divorced, he practiced what he preached. To him, relationship-building and dating one and the same, and he had determined that these were the keys:

- **Smile and look approachable.** As he taught in class, the power of a true smile is contagious and intoxicating.
- **Ask open-ended questions.** Open-ended questions are, in essence, not questions at all, but more request statements. Instead of asking, "What do you do?" Dalton would say, "Tell me about your work or your passion; hopefully they are one and the same!" These types of questions elicit a much more detailed response.
- **70/30 Rule.** Dalton changed this to the 90/10 rule. He was paid to speak. He *loved* to speak. He also knew that he always had plenty of opportunities to speak. Not everyone else did. Every person wants to be heard. Dalton had experienced the phenomenon of being a great listener. Not only does the person you are talking to think you are a great listener, but they really view you as a great conversationalist and you have barely said anything!

Dalton applied this with Lauren and he saw very quickly the problem with her date the previous evening. Her date spent the entire time talking and trying to impress her; she would have been much more impressed with someone who listened to her.

Lauren spoke of her background: how she grew up, attending Stanford on a full soccer scholarship, her father's untimely death due to cancer, and her current role working for Kelli. She raved about Kelli and her leadership. Lauren had one sister, three years younger than Lauren and mentally disabled. Dalton could sense the love she had for her sister the way she talked about Robin. Lauren spoke of Robin's zest for life and how genuinely happy and upbeat she was, regardless of her own short comings. It was very inspirational and Dalton mentioned he hoped to meet her someday.

Suddenly, 8:00 pm had become 11:00 pm with a blink of an eye. That was the telltale sign of a great conversation. The night flew by, there were no awkward pauses, and the conversation transitioned smoothly from topic to topic. Dalton lightly nibbled on the food; he did not want to overeat and he was desperately trying to stay in shape. Meals like this on the road were what really killed him.

They wrapped up close to midnight and said their warm goodbyes to Uncle Gino. (Dalton felt natural calling him this regardless of the newness of their relationship.) Lauren and Dalton each ordered Ubers back home. As Lauren's ride pulled up in front of the restaurant, Dalton thanked her once again. She went in for a warm hug and, while hugging, both leaned left to kiss the other on the cheek. Their lips met surprisingly and each felt the spark of chemistry that they knew was already there. Dalton pulled away after a few seconds and naturally apologized. Lauren smiled, leaned back into Dalton, and kissed him full on the lips. She stated he had nothing to apologize for and rushed off to grab her ride.

The next morning, Dalton was not slated to begin until 11:00 am. This gave him time to prepare his presentation and final review notes of the team's presentations. This included sitting with Mike and making sure they captured everything that was pertinent. Dalton desperately needed a decent night of sleep but that was not going to happen this evening. There was always a trade-off: sleep in or workout. He tended to feel lethargic without his workout so he chose the latter and still planned on being up by 6:30 am to meet with Mike by 8:00 am.

Dalton laid in bed smiling to himself as the exhilaration of a beautiful, intelligent woman coming on to him refused to leave his mind. Since his separation, he had dated many women, a few of whom had seemingly been waiting out his marriage. In every instance, Dalton was the initiator. He correctly read the signs but he initiated. To have such a woman initiate was very flattering. He did not allow himself to get caught up in thoughts of what could be. He still felt uncomfortable about this occurring with someone from a client's office, even though Kelli gave her blessings and he stayed very professional. Regardless, Lauren lived in the Bay Area and he lived a three-hour flight away.

The dating scene for Dalton was limited at best. At first, he got out there a lot. Nice looking, in decent shape, intelligent, but probably most importantly, blessed with the gift of gab. He was always very confident in his ability to charm anyone. That is how his company has grown organically over the past ten years.

Dalton and Mike met for breakfast and walked through how the videos were to be presented to the team. Dalton wanted each in the following order:

- Video without sound
- Video with sound
- Highlights specifically chosen by Dalton

Dalton discovered this order to be very effective for each speaker to review their presentation with their peers. Without sound, everyone spent time focusing only on their body language, facial expressions, movement, and the like. Many idiosyncrasies were caught on this first video review. Next, the team would tend to focus on the voice more than the body movement, but the two were reviewed together. The team should be able to pick up on any tonal inconsistencies and whether appropriate voice inflection was used. Finally, Dalton highlighted a few specific points with each speaker to discuss. This would assist in reiterating some of the key points Dalton picked up on immediately during each presentation.

For the review session, Dalton tended to dress up more. He had not retired his three-piece suits but he tended to a more casual look when speaking. Maybe it was maturity, maybe it was laziness, maybe it was a little bit of frugalness. He knew that any logo gear that was worn served as a marketing (and tax write-off) opportunity. He had many different colors of polos with the company logo. He even went the route of having a matching computer bag and luggage with the company logo. He also used the cover of his MacBook Air as a billboard, with his logo skin on the cover.

Dalton knew the team would look at his presentation skills today as he constructively criticized their presentation skills. He broke out the well-pressed blue pinstripe suit (no jacket, just vest), blue-and-white-checked shirt, and patterned navy blue tie (navy blue is Dalton's power color). He even brought out his chestnut and cream two-toned wing tip shoes, something he has been known for for many years. As he prepared for the review session, he swung by Austin's office to discuss the issue he had mentioned yesterday.

CHAPTER EIGHT

Coaching and Mentoring

D ALTON MEETS WITH Austin, head of Information Technology at Sojo Technologies, to determine the right path and approach to deliver feedback to one of his directors, David Allison. Austin is struggling with David because he was recently promoted to vice president, a role David believes should have been his.

PEOPLE-CENTRIC SKILLS IN THIS CHAPTER

- Coaching and Mentoring Defined
- When to Use Coaching and Mentoring
- What a Combined Coaching and Mentoring Approach Looks Like
- How to Deliver Contentious Feedback

KEY WORDS

- Coaching
- Mentoring
- Feedback

Prior to the team gathering, Dalton stopped by Austin's office as they had discussed the previous evening. Austin looked stressed and Dalton was not sure if it was due to the upcoming team training or the forthcoming issue. Dalton knew this was Austin's first executive management role. After a few minutes of pleasantries, Dalton learned he was struggling with one of his directors, David Allison. David was a man of great intelligence but there was a significant amount of tension between Austin and David. Since Austin was relatively new to this role, Dalton asked the obvious question: was the tension driven by jealousy? Austin was not 100% positive but he thought this had something to do with it. Austin and David had a very productive professional relationship prior to Austin's promotion. In fact, they might have been considered pretty casual friends. They were peers until the promotion. Since then, David had become combative and Austin was concerned that he was becoming a cancer for the team.

David was not supportive but seemed to be passive-aggressive; he never confronted Austin in person but tended to stir the pot with rumors and innuendo. He did his job competently, but didn't add any additional effort in his role. He denied his negative behavior but continued to engage in it. Austin wanted some insight and strategies about how to handle David. David was good enough at his job but, as Austin stated, everyone is replaceable. He has thought of going that route but worried he might lose credibility with the team if he fired David without working through these potential problems. It would be very costly and time-consuming to find a replacement and get them up to speed.

Dalton took a long sip of his iced coffee and thought about ways to assist Austin in handling this delicate issue with David. He considered varying conflict management strategies but thought it was best to focus on coaching and mentoring. Dalton highlighted the differences between the two approaches.

"No matter the area of focus, a coach tends to specialize in improving one or two areas of development at a time, with laserfocus on those areas and then progressively moving to other areas of focus as needed. In general, a coach tutors/instructs/motivates a person to achieve a specific goal or skill. You have executive coaches in corporate America"—Dalton winked and smiled; this was a role he frequently played—"Caleb has his soccer team coach and also has a skills coach when he has one-on-one lessons, and has his strength and conditioning coach as well. Their interaction is planned and structured."

"Based on the technical definitions, mentoring has a varied purpose and goal. A mentor is a trusted counselor or guide.[1] Mentoring is the act of guiding, counseling, and supporting. Mentoring can be packaged with coaching but, in general, this is vastly different from coaching. Fundamentally, this is the

---

[1] https://www.merriam-webster.com/dictionary/mentor

role of a teacher. The objective is where the difference really lies. Mentorship is more voluntary in nature and less formal. The mentor and protégé focus on a broad development goal. Mentoring can encompass many complex areas of development."

In Dalton's opinion, they needed to confront this immediately. It had been going on for far too long (four months) and Dalton was concerned that Austin was losing credibility for allowing this to happen for an extended period. There were a few different stages to the approach Dalton had in mind.

"David is obviously upset that you were promoted instead of him. Does that mean he does not like you, trust you, or respect you?" Austin furrowed his brow and pondered the answer as Dalton continued. "If it's not personal, has it become personal? It sounds like you guys were friends at one time, so let's assume he still likes you. Based on that assumption and based on his behavior, I believe it is a respect/trust factor. He knows you are competent but strongly believes he is more competent. The first step is to attempt to reestablish a trusting relationship. Right now, through no fault of yours, he does not trust you, and this has caused him to doubt your previous relationship, which has led him to a lack of respect.

"In my opinion, we need to use a hybrid of coaching and mentoring to help to resolve this situation and move forward in a productive manner. I smashed the words together and I get *Mentch*, which is a similar pronunciation and meaning to the Yiddish word *mensch*. Mensch is a noun that describes a person of integrity and honor.[2] In essence, that is what you have to become to reestablish trust with David. If he believes you are looking out for his best interests and you will treat him fairly since he believes he was wronged, I think we could make this work."

Dalton finished and peered at Austin to get his thoughts. Austin stated that everything made sense and he was on board so far and supportive of the general direction.

"Effective coaching has to be done in a trusting environment. There is no alternative to this. Trust is the foundation of all strong personal and professional relationships. Coaching will be the first opportunity to demonstrate to him that he can trust you again because you use the coaching session as a tool for building David and the relationship back up and not letting him tear it down. We need to address the issue head-on and state why this coaching session is necessary. Since he is denying his behavior, let's not play that game with him, and say we want to start with a clean slate. Avoid using the coaching session

---

[2] https://dictionary.com/mensh

as a venue to deliver reprimands and bad news. This is not the place for that kind of information. Avoid using coaching when only negative things need to be addressed. Coaching should be a purposeful event that happens regularly and is devoid of negative information. This is not to say we cannot discuss specific performance issues after this initial session. It just has to be presented in a way that speaks to development rather than to punishment. We need to make these coaching sessions a haven for encouragement and development and not a place for stress and discouragement. Without trust, you will not be able to coach well."

Dalton grabbed his MacBook Air out of his backpack and pulled up a slide deck on the topic at hand. He presented Austin with a slide that highlighted seven steps to building trust with employees both in and out of coaching sessions.

Building Trust

1. Maintain positive body language. Some considerations include:
   a. Open gestures tell the other person you are approachable and open to communication. Appropriate hand gestures to show you are drawing team members ideas in will help them know you are paying attention and will keep them.
   b. Good posture will show you are standing at attention, and moving closer to show you are listening intently will make them feel important, but do not impede their personal space or they will feel intimidated or threatened.
   c. Open posture will show the other person you are open to feedback and moving forward.
   d. When delivering constructive feedback, lean away from the person you are delivering the feedback to. Consider leaning at an angle and lessen eye contact so the person can absorb the feedback without someone gazing at them. If you lean back, this will lessen the blow and come off as less aggressive.
   e. By leaning your head to the side after delivering feedback, it shows interest in their response and empathy for their response.
2. Employ the 70/30 rule. Listening gives the other person a voice. Having a voice helps to build trust. Focused, active listening is key.
3. Always respect your team members. Respect is foundational to trust.

4. Keep things confidential. If they do not feel they can tell you anything, they will never open up. If you cannot keep the information being presented as confidential, then state that ahead of time.

5. Keep your promises. Broken promises equate to broken trust. When you say, "You have my word," you had better mean it.

6. Be honest and transparent. Provide candid, tactfully direct feedback and be as transparent as possible. Transparency builds trust.

7. Tell them you believe in them. In order for an employee to trust their supervisor, they need to know they are supported. By telling them you believe in them, it will continue to rebuild trust.

Dalton was excited that they would broached the topic of body language during the presentation skills session later in the morning. Dalton and Austin bantered on the topic as Austin captured the salient points.

Dalton continued on how to be a Mentch and blend both coaching and mentoring. "There is no right or wrong answer when determining which aspects you may want to combine. Pick the pieces that will help you achieve maximum results," Dalton stated. For example, in this instance, Dalton considered it prudent to blend the relationship-building aspect of mentoring to the planned meeting intervals. Some of the benefits realized when combining coaching with mentorship include:

- Increased flexibility
- Supervise while acting autonomous
- Empowers David to make the decision whether he wants to continue and be successful in this environment or take a different path
- David will think he is empowered in the path he takes
- Enlist the assistance of other managers in the management of David as necessary

Blending the two models provides more flexibility with the monitoring Austin will need to ensure David is developing while reestablishing trust and support moving forward.

Dalton and Austin discussed the approach Austin was planning on utilizing with David:

- Discuss (in-person) with David:
  - David understands he was very deserving of Austin's position.

- That is not what happened so we are at a crossroads.
- What can Austin do to help David move past this?
- What are David's long-term goals at the company?
- Are there any projects he would like to be in charge of?
- How can Austin help him get there?
- Discuss some of the rumors that Austin has heard; he believes someone is trying to stir the pot but is moving forward with a clean slate.
- Ask for David's assistance on creating a positive culture for the rest of the team.
- Give David the opportunity to elevate to Austin's official number two.

Dalton thought Austin could handle this on his own but could definitely see the hesitation and some semblance of lack of confidence in having this discussion one-one-one, so Dalton suggested that he could attend under the guise of working with Austin as an executive coach. Dalton would be there to help Austin, rather than to manage David. Austin emphatically loved the idea and set up some time with David for the next morning. Dalton stopped by prior to the team training and looped Kelli in on the plan and she was 100% on board.

CHAPTER NINE

Presentation Skills and Body Language

D ALTON REVIEWS THE videos completed by Kelli's team and delivers feedback to the team on presentation skills and body language and other topics that assist in delivering a top-notch presentation.

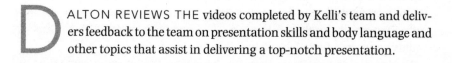

PEOPLE-CENTRIC SKILLS IN THIS CHAPTER

- Leading practices in presentation skills and building effective presentation materials
- How to win over an audience quickly
- Ending a presentation effectively and other little things that can be immediately implemented to improve presentations
- Leading practices in reading body language

KEY WORDS

- Presentation Skills
- Public Speaking
- Body Language
- Gesture Clusters

After chatting with Austin, Dalton had 15 minutes prior to the team meeting. He needed this time to focus mentally and to home in on the rest of the afternoon. Dalton was very excited to see the team walk into the conference room a few minutes before 11:00 am. He rarely had his headphones on in the workplace but, before speaking in front of a group, he enjoyed zoning out and getting lost in the music. His playlist was an eclectic mix of many genres and eras. In the 15 minutes before class, he strolled through a little Thin Lizzy ("Cowboy Song"), Def Leppard ("High 'n' Dry"), Robyn ("Handle Me"), and ended with Queen ("Don't Stop Me Now"). These were a few of the songs that provided the energy, focus, and enthusiasm for the rest of the day.

He was deep in his own thoughts, concentrating on updating his task list and calendar on the computer, and did not see Angela and Jeffrey walk in. He looked up to their mild smirking—when focused, Dalton tended to lip-sync the lyrics. He was very comfortable in his own shoes, in who and what he is, so he took the smirking in jest. One aspect he planned to discuss with Austin was being comfortable with himself and making sure he knows who he is. Dalton knew this firsthand, because once he had attained this, his business and speaking career took off.

Rodger arrived shortly after, followed by Lauren and Austin. Lauren walked powerfully, smiling brightly. Dalton had been unsure if her behavior would change but it wholeheartedly did not.

Prior to taking the team through the videos, Dalton spent some time on basic presentation skills that would help the team moving forward.

 ## CREATING AN OUTLINE

Dalton strongly believed in the power of a well-ordered outline, so he walked the team through creating a basic outline for any presentation. The outline serves to organize thoughts, and an audience will get more out of a presentation when it is well organized. He knew the team did not specifically do this yesterday, but he figured they might have roughly thought it through to organize their presentations.

In general, a good outline starts with the skeleton—the basics, the bare minimum of the speech in a form that loosely resembles the shape it will eventually take—and progresses by adding details to the skeleton (the "meat") and layering the rest on top of that. At key points of the presentation, specific issues will need to be confronted, and allotting them a place in the basic outline ensures that these are prioritized and addressed correctly.

ORGANIZING THE PRESENTATION

Using an outline, these basic parts of a presentation should be considered:

- **Opening:** Some speakers like to begin with a joke (like Jeffrey from the previous day). This starts the presentation on a light note and puts the audience at ease, reducing any unnecessary tension for both the audience and the speaker. But this can be a dangerous tactic if the joke does not go over well. If a presentation starts with something that does not click, the audience may question your ability as a speaker. Dalton loves humor and likes to start out with something light. On the occasion that the joke bombs, he then follows up with some self-deprecating humor:
  - "Not sure if you knew this, but you guys were supposed to laugh!"
  - "That was a joke!"
  - "Tough crowd!"

  This seemed to work well for him. Other ways to start include asking a rhetorical question, giving people a surprising statistic, or telling a brief anecdote related to the topic. Dalton continually found ways to personalize the topical material. His stories might be lengthy but they were reliably humorous or highlighted a key point. He always managed to wind it back to the topic at hand.
- **Body:** The body supports all key points introduced in the opening. These are your supporting arguments. Think about a presentation as something tangible that is left behind. Audiences tend to remember random bits of information. Throwaway lines you assume will pass over people's heads may end up being the bits that certain people recall, so be sure to keep a close eye on what you say and how you say it.

  Often, people make the mistake of believing that the more they say, the better their speech is. Dalton has time and time again dispelled this notion. Others, feeling that brevity is key to being viewed as witty, keep what they say to a minimum. As with everything, the truth lies in between, and the key to making a presentation powerful and wellreceived is to deliver a message with conviction and say enough to support your key points without going over your time allotment. There is no point in extending a presentation with extraneous detail that no one will remember and that, in fact, will distract from the key messages.

- **Review:** Restate key points briefly for those who might have "tuned out" the first time you made them.

- **Closing:** Restate the main point of your presentation. In some cases, you may want to give people a call to action. Dalton reminded the audience always to close last and end with their key points.

The amount of time given to each section of a presentation is governed by how much time you have overall and how much of that time will be necessary to get all of your points across.

Audiences can be skeptical about a speaker's message, especially if the speaker is addressing a potentially controversial issue. Credibility is built with an audience by using reliable sources of information and supporting statements with citations to trusted authorities.

Once you have outlined your speech and lined up solid evidence to back up key ideas, it is time to pull all of the pieces together. Do not have everything you want to say written down; pulling together a series of ideas or prompts (via PowerPoint) is the most effective method of structuring notes. If you read from a script, then there is significantly less of a chance you'll be convincing and get your point across with the power that you want to have.

CREATING A PRESENTATION

Presentations should be viewed as social occasions. Dalton always viewed each presentation as a performance. He did not admit that to many people; he thought it was pretty cheesy. Regardless, it helped to get him focused on the task at hand. Effective speakers need to connect with their audience—not a connection like the one Lauren and Dalton seemed to have, but they need to connect on some level.

Try to personalize the experience. Reading a speech monotonously word for word creates a barrier between the speaker and the audience and eliminates spontaneity. Everyone should feel like you are having a conversation with them, not lecturing them. Speeches should come alive with your words and presentation. The best speakers have minimal notes and present fluidly, naturally. This allows them to develop rapport with the audience, maintain eye contact, and gives the words more resonance. Speech readers tend to hold questions till the end because it is difficult to respond to questions that may arise in the course of your presentation.

In order to help calm any nerves, if you feel writing out part of your speech is necessary, the best thing to do is to create an elevator pitch for your speech. Map out the first minute or so, similar to the way football teams script the first ten plays so they can understand what the defense is going to throw at them to start the game.

Dalton also discussed the importance of being flexible. Things go wrong; stuff is bound to happen. It is almost inevitable that at some point you will encounter unexpected problems in giving presentations. How you handle adversity shows people who you truly are. People get flustered when bad stuff happens. They may become irritated or flustered. The audience picks up on the negative emotion quickly and can form a negative impression of the speaker. Artful speakers treat unexpected problems humorously. This puts everyone at ease and starts to build a rapport with the audience. This is one element that separates comfortable public speakers from speakers who are less professional.

Having the confidence to turn them into something that can drive a presentation forward is the mark of a good speaker.

BEING PREPARED

Preparedness is key to mastering any skill. Practice makes perfect, but there is such a thing as being overprepared. Being prepared serves many purposes, but most importantly it gives you the self-confidence to get up in front of many people. There's famous quote attributed to Benjamin Franklin: "It is often said that those who fail to plan, plan to fail." Preparing helps lessen any nerves and should help minimize any obvious or elementary issues.

CHECKING OUT THE VENUE

When Dalton speaks at large conferences (over 1,000 attendees), he likes to understand the spacing where he will be presenting. Dalton walked the venue and recommended others do so because this was part of preparing. Some things to look for include:

- Is there room to walk around the room throughout the presentation?
- Is there a podium?
- Is there a raised stage?
- What equipment is available?

There might be other considerations but Dalton focused on specifics that would help distinguish his speakers. Dalton smiled when talking about the podium and glanced at Lauren because he knew what was to come in the video reviews. He discussed the importance of not hiding from the audience behind the podium. He recommended not to have any physical barriers so as not to be tempted to use them.

OVERCOMING NERVOUSNESS AND PREPARING MENTALLY: BEFORE THE PRESENTATION

Caleb is a nervous wreck before soccer games. He has gotten better but for many years his stomach would start to hurt and he vomited routinely before games (and sometimes even during the game!). Dalton always told Caleb that it is okay to be nervous. Being nervous highlights how important something is to you. Once Dalton got this through to Caleb, this fact seemed to naturally calm him. Additionally, nervousness causes adrenaline to be released into the blood, sending impulses to organs to create a specific response.[1] Adrenaline causes a noticeable increase in strength and performance, in addition to heightened awareness during stress.[2] Too much adrenaline can be damaging but nerves are natural.

Nervousness can create unwanted physical reactions, including feeling queasy, sweating profusely, sweaty palms, and a dry throat, among others.

Channel your nervousness by forcing yourself to speak clearly and to make eye contact with your listeners. Balance is important in delivering any presentation. The audience will reflect your emotion. If you come across as too relaxed, you could sound a bit bored. If you are bored, then the audience will expect to be bored as well, and they will need very little excuse to check out and not listen to you.

Dalton never thought much of mental preparation. What he found out is that he regularly prepared mentally but just did not view it as preparing mentally. Working out, yoga, listening to music, meditation—Dalton did all of these routinely. All of these are a big part of mental preparation but the key is to figure out what works best for you.

---

[1] https://www.hormone.org/your-health-and-hormones/glands-and-hormones-a-to-z/hormones/adrenaline
[2] Ibid.

Like a professional athlete preparing for a big game, you need to keep yourself in a positive frame of mind as you prepare for your own big event. Dalton walked everyone though a list of potential mental preparations exercises.

- **Exercise.** If you are someone who enjoys physical or mental exercise, stay in your routine and do it the night before or morning of. Dalton worked out religiously because he enjoyed it but he knew lethargy would set in without his workout.
- **Eat Right.** Eating light or healthy is key to continuing to build strong self-confidence. Not only that, but certain foods will make you feel tired or lethargic.
- **Sleep.** Dalton was not a big sleeper. In fact, he abhorred sleeping and considered it a waste of time. Part of this was due to his ex-wife, who *loved* to sleep. That being said, Dalton realized the importance of getting a good six to seven hours of sleep every night. If he did not get his sleep, he would tend to drink too much caffeine and become jittery and would not eat as healthy as he should.
- **Hydration.** Dry mouth can happen to any speaker. Staying hydrated and having water available will help combat that.
- **Chew Gum.** Jaw movement can help release nervous energy. Research has shown an increased vigilance, a lower level of anxiety, a decrease in the experience of stress, and a lower elevation of cortisol levels when people chew gum.[3] Caleb has coped with stress and focus issues in school by chewing gum. In fact, his doctor gave him a note for school to allow him to chew gum and the teachers observed a notable improvement in his focus level.

OVERCOMING NERVOUSNESS AND PREPARING MENTALLY: DURING THE PRESENTATION

- **Breath**. Progressive breathing before, during, and even after your presentation is key. Deep breathing is one of the best ways to lower stress in the body. When you breathe deeply, it sends a message to your brain to calm down and relax.[4] The brain then passes this message on to the body.

---

[3] https://www.skillsyouneed.com/present/presentation-nerves.html
[4] https://www.uofmhealth.org/health-library/uz2255

Indicators of stress (increased heart rate, high blood pressure, etc.) all decrease when you breathe deeply.[5]

- **Slow Down/Pause**. Nerves tend to make everyone speak faster. There are a few ways to slow down, including pausing. Using pauses or silence is one of the most effective speaking techniques. (Ironic, to say the least.) Appropriate pausing emphasizes a key point that was just said. This gives the audience a moment to absorb the message. Dalton learned to speak with rhythm and that seemed to help calm his nerves. He would tend to sing his words (to an extent) in order to make sure there were pauses throughout.
- **Movement.** Moving around throughout a presentation will help use some of that nervous energy. There are numerous other benefits of movement during a presentation but this is primary from the perspective of managing nerves. Moving throughout could take the primary attention of the attendees off you and on your slides or other peripherals. That is not the long-term goal but might help during moments of stress.

When Liora performed in school plays, Dalton would have her focus on the path she has taken more than the actual performance. The work is done; you have practiced, you are prepared, and the rest is the icing on the cake. Liora does have anxiety, which seems to have become more evident over the past few years. She is nervous about everything: school, friends, going anywhere, and so on. Dalton always warns her of becoming a self-fulfilling prophecy: if you think nerves will mess you up, nerves will mess you up. He reiterates his message to Caleb as well: nerves are natural when something is important.

Dalton began to take the team through the videos, in the order he previously specified:

- Video without sound
- Video with sound
- Highlights specifically highlighted by Dalton

Everyone intently watched the videos, even though they were a little confused at first by watching the videos without sound. It quickly became evidently what they could pick up on without sound. Dalton intermingled teaching moments and slides with the video reviews. It could be challenging to shift from slides to video to discussion and back and forth but this was second nature to Dalton; he transitioned smoothly.

---

[5] Ibid.

APPEARING CONFIDENT IN FRONT OF THE CROWD

Throughout the videos, Dalton highlighted when each team member appeared more or less confident. The team was able to pick up on this relatively easily. Someone who exudes confidence demonstrates certain characteristics:

- No notes or notecards (in hands). Notes are used as a crutch at times and, as previously mentioned, in many cases, speakers forget about the notes and they are not used.
- Being well-organized can also improve your self-confidence.
- Smiling is a surefire way to gain engagement and lessen nerves.

The most important thing to remember in order to deliver the most confident presentation is awareness of your surroundings.

DELIVERING YOUR SPEECH

After watching the first 30 seconds of each video, Dalton paused and walked the group through some ways to make sure a presentation starts off with the right tone.

- **Start off strong by preparing an opening that will capture the audience's attention.** What do they care about? What is going to grab their attention?
- **Check the volume of your voice.** Do you need a microphone? Does your voice carry or is it timid? A powerful, friendly voice will garner the attention of the audience immediately.
- **Smile.** Smiling is one of the key aspects to engaging people and eliciting questions and feedback.

The opening should be very brief, in most cases one to two minutes (scripting out the first part, as previously mentioned). In that short span of time, you should present yourself and your topic in a way that will make your audience want to pay attention. A few different ways to approach this include:

- **Traditional.** Start out with one to two minutes on the topic at hand; introduce the topic and the key supporting points that will reiterate the topic.

- **Questioning.** Start out with a question related to the topic that, based on their answers and discussion, naturally leads the group back to the key topic.
- **Dialogue.** Similar to Questioning, start with a discussion, but not necessarily a question.
- **Controversial.** This approach is a little trickier and not necessarily for a novice speaker. Start out with a statement that is opposite of your main topic. This will get the audience engaged and enthusiastic, but you have to reel them back in relatively quickly. Controversial in this manner is more to do with slight differences of opinion than saying something that will offend people. For example, try opening with a statement along the lines of "Here is something that I do not theoretically believe is necessary." Follow this up by saying, "You may not agree with me, but give me a chance to prove this to you here and now."

An effective opening conveys to your audience that what you are going to say will be interesting and will get their attention. Dalton smirked when he discussed this because it reminded him of the movie *How to Lose a Guy in 10 Days*, the 2003 movie starring Kate Hudson and Matthew McConaughey. Although he did not remember much about the movie, it gave him the concept "How to Lose an Audience in the First Two Minutes":

- Stand behind the podium the entire beginning of the presentation.
- Start out with a whimper.
- Tell the audience you are new at this.
- Tell the audience this not your best topic.
- Do not smile.
- Do not command the audience.

 FLEXIBILITY IS KEY!

Dalton focuses on teaching his speakers the importance of flexibility. He believes this is so important that he mentions it numerous times during training sessions. "You might speak on the same topic many times in a year but no presentation will ever be the same!" Based on the current of the presentation, audience dialogue, and questions, presentations will take on many different ebbs and flows. Additionally, it is very important to read the audience to make sure they stay engaged. Audiences can lose interest for many reasons. Some ways to reengage them include:

- Ask questions. Dalton made it a point to learn the names of as many attendees as possible so he could engage them on a personal level. He was fond of saying, "People always listen for one word no matter what: their name!" Knowing attendee names is key to engagement.
- Have a member of the audience come to the front of the room and help you with a demonstration. Having people get involved is a great way to reengage.
- Conduct a straw poll and take opinions from both sides to start a topic of discussion.
- Introduce a brief, interesting digression (go off topic for two or three minutes). Anybody who knew Dalton well knew that he was an open book. He digressed into his personal life all the time. The key was making sure the story correlated at least a little to the topic at hand. People enjoy this personal approach, especially when the topic might be a little dry and this livens it up a bit.
- Use a brief anecdote (preferably one that has something to do with your topic). Same as above: use your personal experiences but be able to wind back to the key topic.

Each of the above strategies offers a change of pace, and if your audience has given the appearance of losing interest, these can turn things around by reminding the audience that there is a reason for them to listen and it might actually be enjoyable!

 ## COMMUNICATING WITH BODY LANGUAGE

In 1967, the *Journal of Consulting Psychology* published a study[6] conducted by UCLA researchers that would help better understand the importance of nonverbal communication. Written by UCLA professor Albert Mehrabian and Susan R. Ferris, the piece described the relative importance of words, tone of voice, and body language in understanding an underlying emotional message.[7]

---

[6] http://changingminds.org/explanations/behaviors/body_language/mehrabian.htm
[7] https://www.lifesize.com/en/video-conferencing-blog/speaking-without-words

Subjects were given three recordings of the word "maybe," conveying three emotions (disfavor, favor, and neutrality). Next, they were shown photos of female faces expressing the same three emotions and were asked to determine the emotions of both the recordings and the photos. The participants accurately guessed the emotion conveyed in the photos by a margin of 3:2.[8]

In a second study, subjects listened to recordings of nine words with different tones (positive, neutral, and negative):

- Affection ("honey," "thanks," and "dear")
- Neutrality ("oh," "really," and "maybe")
- Dislike ("don't," "terrible," and "brute")

Not surprisingly, the response to each word was dependent more on the inflection of the voice than the connotation of the word itself. Dr. Mehrabian devised a formula to describe how the mind determines meaning. He concluded that the interpretation of a message is 7% verbal, 38% vocal, and 55% visual. The conclusion was that 93% of communication is "nonverbal" in nature.[9] Nonverbal communication impacts every facet of our life. The impact is massive but most people do not fully understand how to interpret body language.

THE POWER OF BODY LANGUAGE

Understanding body language will not only improve relationships but will help you understand what is around you and what language your body is speaking. Body language can be very powerful in several ways:

- **Bitter Honesty:** Body language can convey truth, even when words might not.
- **Self-Awareness:** Understanding body language can help you understand your own actions that might stop your own success.
- **Understand Feelings:** Body language shows feelings and motive.
- **Enhance Listening and Communication Skills:** Paying attention to body language makes better listeners. Listening not only takes the ears; you can listen immensely with your eyes.

---

[8] Ibid.
[9] https://www.lifesize.com/en/video-conferencing-blog/speaking-without-words

READING BODY LANGUAGE

Since Dalton started consulting, he progressively became adept at reading body language. Similar to improving listening skills, Dalton did not perceive it to be tricky or difficult. He always said that just by trying harder and focusing, anyone can become a good listener and be good at reading body language. It may take a bit of effort but it is easy to get pretty good at reading body language. In fact, you might already be good at it without being aware of it.

Dalton attempted to have a very light and fun atmosphere in class. He tried to make sure everyone interacted throughout the day. He enjoyed using games in class and funny cartoons and pictures, including pictures of his kids. He pulled up a slide to introduce the body language section with a cartoon of Caleb in a similar pose to the Vitruvian Man by Leonardo da Vinci.

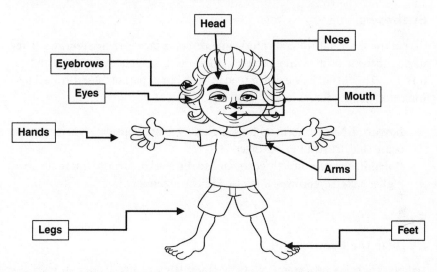

Head

The position of a person's head can be a surefire and easy-to-read indicator of emotion. Some key considerations relate to movement and position:

- **Nodding:** Nodding typically indicates agreement to what has been said. The speed of the nod can have varying meanings. A faster nod could signal impatience, a gentler one could mean appreciation and interest, and a slow nod can be a sign of interest or a polite, fake signal. Look to the eyes for confirmation.

- **Head Firm/Head Up:** Person is listening with an open mind and without bias.
- **Head Fully Down:** Opposite of head up, this position indicates disinterest or rejection of what is said (possibly keeping quiet to avoid conflict).
- **Tilted to the Side:** This means a person is thoughtful or possibly considering what is being said.
- **Head High:** Holding the head high signals extreme confidence or feeling of superiority.
- **Chin Up:** The chin up indicates defiance, extreme confidence, or potentially arrogance.
- **Head Forward:** Head leaning forward directly indicates interest.
- **Head Tilted Down:** Tilting the head down signals disapproval, distrust, or potentially doubt.[10]

Eyebrows

One of the most natural indicators on a person's face is their eyebrows. They move subconsciously with a person's emotions. Like all body language indicators, they should not be viewed or read in a silo but as part of the entire package. Indicators to look for include:

- **Lowered:** Numerous meanings, including focus, consideration for what is being said, frustration, or anger.
- **Raised:** Surprise, directly correlated to the level of surprise (more surprise, higher raised eyebrows). Can also indicate openness.[11]

Eyes

It's All in the Eyes

Dalton is a huge proponent of eye contact. His parents always stressed the importance of eye contact when he was a child. His mother told him adults would be nicer to him and respect him if he could hold eye contact (in addition to having a good handshake). His mother was born in Egypt and grew up in Paris; his father was born in Poland. All of these cultures, in addition to the North American culture he grew up in, stressed the importance of eye contact in developing strong relationships and, most importantly, trust. People give a

---

[10] https://www.tutorialspoint.com/body_language/body_language_head_positions.htm
[11] http://changingminds.org/techniques/body/parts_body_language/eyebrows_body_language.htm

great deal away through their eyes. The eyes are an important factor when reading a person's body language. Dalton mentioned a few specifics to look for when reading a person's eyes:

- **Peering to the Left:** Eyes in this direction can mean someone is remembering something or recollecting facts (based on which hand is dominant, as previously mentioned). Peering to the left and downward can indicate self-communication and peering left without looking down could mean an internal conversation is occurring. When Dalton traveled for business he was almost always alone, and he definitely knew that he had many internal conversations where his eyes would peer left. Sometimes he had these internal conversations out loud and he would receive many odd looks from people overhearing this!
- **Looking Sideways:** Looking sideways and to the right is associated with imagination (by reading neurolinguistic programming) and may mean a story. Looking sideways and to the left is potentially the exact opposite of imagination. In most cases, it means you are accessing memory and remembering a story.
- **Looking to the Right:** As previously mentioned, looking to the right indicates imagination. It can mean guessing or lying. If you combine looking right with looking down, it means there could be a self-question. On the other hand, if you combine looking right with looking up, it can mean lying.
- **Direct Eye Contact:** When speaking, specifically in North America, this means sincerity and honesty. When listening, it indicates interest in the conversation at hand. Dalton had used this to his advantage for many years now. He knew eye contact and listening were game changers.
- **Wide Eyes:** The widening of the eyes or the furrowing of the brows (discussed above) signal wonder or surprise. Dalton experienced this directly when he told his ex-wife Leslie that he would acquiesce and move forward with their separation. When she suggested this to Dalton, she initially thought he would say he did not want it. That was always his reaction. This one was different.
- **Rolled Eyes:** The rolling of the eyes is a universal symbol of disbelief and possibly frustration. This can be viewed as hostile and rude.
- **Blinking:** Frequent blinking can indicate excitement. On the other hand, infrequent blinking could mean extreme boredom or extreme concentration, depending focus. This is the perfect example of making sure, when

reading body language, to take in the entire picture and not overfocus on one part.
- **Winking:** Winking is a friendly gesture or secret joke, possibly indicating mischief.
- **Rubbing Eyes:** Rubbing eyes may be caused by tiredness. It can also indicate disbelief or frustration.

Many years ago, Dalton had a very unique experience with an eye-roller. A young woman in class (Deidre, a name he would never forget, based on this experience) at a new client continued to roll her eyes in class one day. This was the first of two days in class with this sales team. Even when she gave him a semi-smile and chuckled at a joke or a comment, the eyes were still rolling. This cause much confusion for Dalton. He was not sure if she was doing this purposefully or if was her natural reaction (an uncontrollable reaction). He chatted with Barbara, the head of sales, after the first day and she was very apologetic. Barbara answered his question on Deidre, shaking her head, peering downward in disappointment. "Dalton, I am so sorry you have to deal with this. This has been a recurring issue since she started with us. We have her on a PIP (Performance Improvement Plan) and this is something that has been called out by employees, managers, and potential clients. I will talk with her." Dalton did not mention this because he was offended; he mentioned it because he knew it would be a problem with clients.

The next day, Deidre was not in class. She called in sick. He asked Barbara about it and she mentioned that she had spoken to Deidre, who said she would not be in for the day because she was not feeling well. Fast-forward two weeks and Dalton received an email and then certified mail from Deidre's lawyer. She accused Dalton of a violation of certain rights and harassment, which was unfounded and ridiculous on so many levels. He called Barbara and she was apologetic and contrite, sorry he had to deal with this. He never heard from the lawyer again (nor did he expect to) and he did find out the lawyer was Deidre's husband! This incident reiterated the importance of eye contact and having a strong ability to read people's eyes, even if it gets you into hot water sometimes.

Nose

Flared: Can indicate frustration or displeasure.
Wrinkled: Can indicate a distasteful comment, not satisfied with own ideas.
Rubbing/Feeling It: Could indicate someone is not telling the truth or disagreement.[12]

---

[12] http://changingminds.org/techniques/body/parts_body_language/nose_body_language.htm

Mouth

The mouth is also a key indicator of body language. Reading the face can lead you to reading the full picture and supporting the initial indicators or changing your opinion based on additional information.

Turned Up/Down: Otherwise known as a smile or frown!

Pursed Lips: Disapproval/Distrust.

Covering the Mouth: When this occurs, the person is literally embarrassed by the words coming out of their mouth so they cover it to conceal it. Could show embarrassment or distrust.

Lip Biting: Could indicate nervousness or anxiousness.[13]

Facial Expressions

Facial expressions are an important part of body language and the first indicator of someone's mood. While some facial expressions are cultural, some are universal. Understanding the basics of facial expressions and decoding them will help you facilitate better communication.

Many studies that have reviewed the universality of emotions through facial expressions directly link these expressions to specific emotions:

- **Happiness:** More than a smile is needed to indicate happiness. Genuine happiness should include the eyes. Eyelids can crinkle, and when smiling brightly, the eyebrows are naturally raised.
- **Anger:** A frown typically accompanies anger. Additionally, the eyes narrow, the chin points forward, and the eyebrows tend to furrow.
- **Fear:** Wide eyes and slightly raised eyebrows signal fear. (This is similar to surprise, so they can be hard to distinguish.). The lips may be parted or stretched when the mouth is closed, as if the person is sucking in air due to the fear.
- **Surprise:** Surprise is similar to fear. The eyebrows become fully raised and the eyes are wide with surprise. The mouth is usually open.
- **Sadness:** The mouth turns down (frown) when someone is sad. A crease in the forehead and quivering chin accompany this slight frown, in addition to slightly furrowed eyebrows.

---

[13] https://www.verywellmind.com/understand-body-language-and-facial-expressions-4147228

- **Disgust:** The expression of disgust includes the nose. The nose wrinkles or flares, the lips part, and the eyes narrow.

A flash of emotion will typically unconsciously appear on your face, even when you attempt to keep your feelings in check.

Hands

Tightly Clenched Hands: Can indicate someone under undue pressure. In many cases, people do this without realizing it when in a confrontation or conflict.

Standing and Joining Hands Behind Back: Indicates superiority or authority.

Open Hands/Palms Up: Speaking with hands open usually means openness and trustworthiness.

Palms Down: Indicates rigidity or defiance.

Rubbing Hands Together: Shows anticipation.

Clasping Hands/Squeezing Hands: Could mean someone is uncomfortable, nervous, or potentially scared.

Arms and Legs

Crossed Arms/Legs: Potentially signals defensiveness. Physical barrier to the person you are talking to.

Open Arms/Extended: Shows openness and acceptance.

Feet

Pointing Toward: Shows interest.

Tapping/Moving: Indicates impatience.

Dalton finished walking through each aspect of body language and called out the most important and readable pieces of each. He then began to discuss putting all of these pieces together into gesture clusters. "Gestures are dependent upon one another and these formulate a complete picture of what a person is thinking or seeing. These are the gesture clusters. Some simple examples include clusters that indicate Openness, Defensiveness, Evaluation, Nervousness, or Boredom/Impatience." Let's look at each.

In general, body language is considered as being either open or closed. Many different reasons could cause either open or closed body language.

Open body language can come from interest, confidence, aggression, or even relaxation. Closed body language can be caused by defensiveness, the desire to hide or protect oneself, or just simply being cold. Body language can be easy to read but can as easily be misread. Dalton stressed to everyone that the key to body language is having a baseline. "If you know how someone normally behaves from a body language perspective, you can look for changes or inconsistencies. Someone who is cold natured could have extreme closed or defensive body language as their norm. In order to read body language correctly, you need to take everything into account—specifically, the sum of the gesture clusters, or you are bound to misread someone."

Openness

- Open Hands/Posture
- Leaning Forward
- Uncrossed Legs/Arms
- Smiling

On the opposite end of the spectrum, open body language is just that: open (Figure 9.1). Legs not crossed, arms to your side or used in conversation indicate interest and openness. Similar indications can be used with the hands. Open hands tend to keep the communication of body language open, in addition to everything mentioned above.

FIGURE 9.1   Gesture cluster: openness.

FIGURE 9.2   Gesture cluster: defensiveness.

Defensiveness

- Rigidity
- Arms/Legs Tightly Crossed
- Eyes Glancing/Darting Sideways
- Minimal Eye Contact
- Lips Pursed
- Fists Clenched
- Downcast Head

Any time an object or space is put in front of a person, that tends to be viewed as closed off (Figure 9.2). Crossing your arms, sitting with your legs crossed, or hunching forward is viewed as intensely closed-off body language. Sometimes you see people with hypermobility who not only cross their legs but hook one leg behind the other; this could be viewed as very closed off. Additionally, if you place your arms or an object in front of you, this may be a protective measure and could be read as nervousness. Crossing your legs when standing can signify insecurity when combined with crossed arms.

Hands can be read as well. When in distress or conflict, hands tend to be balled up in fists or raised up, as if to signal to the other person to stop.

Please note: It is important to understand how people could misread your body language. If you are cold-natured, your body language could be read as defensiveness.

Evaluation

- Tilted Head
- Hand to Cheek
- Leaning Forward
- Chin Stroking
- Eye Squinted

Most people tend to have a distinct look when considering what was just said or pondering how to respond. (See Figure 9.3.)

Nervousness

- Clearing Throat
- Covering Mouth with Hand
- Tapping Fingers
- Whistling
- Jingling Pocket Change
- Fidgeting
- Twitching Lips/Face

We all have many unconscious gestures that can signal how we are feeling or what we are thinking. (See Figure 9.4.) Nonverbal signals that are completely

FIGURE 9.3 Gesture cluster: evaluation.

FIGURE 9.4 Gesture cluster: nervousness.

unconscious, such as very subtle shifts in the expression of the eyes or body positioning, are integral to understanding communication because these are impossible to fake. They are generated by thoughts and attitudes beyond our conscious volition or control.[14] Some unconscious gestures that many people have include:

- **Nail Biting:** This could indicate nervousness or insecurity.
- **Turning Away:** Looking away from someone who is speaking indicates that you do not believe what they are saying.
- **Pulling Ears:** Tugging at your ears can indicate indecision.
- **Head Tilt:** A brief head tilt means interest. Holding a tilt could mean boredom or lack of understanding.
- **Open Palms:** Showing your palms is a sign of innocence or sincerity.
- **Rubbing Hands Together:** Rubbing your hands together is a sign of excitement or anticipation.
- **Touching Your Chin:** This can indicate that a decision is being made or you are considering what is being said.
- **Hand on Your Cheek:** Touching your cheek can mean someone is thinking.
- **Drumming of fingers:** This is a sign of impatience or boredom.
- **Touching Your Nose:** People often associate touching the nose with potentially lying. It can also signal doubt or rejection.

---

[14] https://www.alchemyassistant.com/topics/Ga2PExi7SUFMgjaD.html

FIGURE 9.5   Gesture cluster: boredom/impatience.

These are not only nervous ticks but can highlight the importance of understanding body language.

Boredom/Impatience

- Drumming of Fingers
- Cupping the Head in the Palm of the Hand
- Foot Swinging
- Looking at Your Watch Obsessively
- Turning Your Body and/or Peering at Exit

When someone is disinterested in the topic or does not want to be there at that moment, they will show signs of boredom or impatience. (See Figure 9.5.) Similar to nervousness, these gestures can be subconscious.

 ## BODY LANGUAGE MISTAKES

Dalton always stresses that there are many different factors that will create false body language signals. This is why it is so important to examine the positions and gestures as a whole when attempting to interpret body language; do not overfocus on one small piece of a large, intricate picture.

Poor Posture

Posture can lead to unfair judgments and prejudices. Often, poor posture is seen as a closed body language that people assume is caused by defensiveness or a lack of confidence. There are, however, many different reasons why someone can have poor posture. Again, do not overfocus on one gesture or single aspect of body language. For example, from his many years in school and corporate America, Dalton developed less than optimal posture from sitting in front of a computer. This is something he constantly worked on but it was still less than optimal.

Invading Personal Space

Depending on the culture you are from and the culture you are in, the amount of personal space in a conversation can vary, but there are general guidelines in Western societyes. Invading personal space is seen as an act of intimidation or potential hostility. There have been many studies on personal space zones, indicating four (or sometimes five) zones:[15]

- **Intimate:** 0 to 24 inches. This space is reserved for intimate relationships, close friends, people who truly care for each other.
- **Personal:** 24 inches to 4 feet. Appropriate for private discussions between small parties.
- **Social:** 4 to 12 feet. Appropriate for public and social conversations. Spacing is relatively open to allow for others to join the conversation.
- **Public:** More than 12 feet. Routinely used for public speeches and important figures; assists in establishing authority.

Dalton reiterated to the group that personal space could vary greatly based on many different factors. Culture, background, and situation can all impact personal space greatly. At times, people will impede personal space to emphasize a key point or to come off aggressive or intimidating. Dalton strongly felt that in Western societies appropriate spacing was very important and mostly adhered to in the workplace. Culture could drive some issues but, in most cases, people who impede personal space in a conversation do so on purpose.

How should you handle a close talker who is impeding your personal space deliberately? The natural reaction is to back up, but this is definitely not the best way to handle someone impeding your personal space. Why? If you back

---

[15] https://atworkjax.wordpress.com/2012/04/09/the-four-zones-of-interpersonal-space/

up, someone doing this purposefully will continue to push forward. If you move back, it is an acknowledgment that the tactic of impeding personal space is working.

What are the other options? You could stand your ground and have a conversation without much space, which might be too close for comfort. Dalton's recommended option is to continue the conversation but reposition yourself while talking and move kitty-corner or slightly to the side. This will give you more space without acknowledging the person is impeding your personal space. This has worked wonders in these situations for Dalton and many people he has recommended this tactic to.

COMMUNICATING WITH POWER

Dalton turned his attention to overall communication and focused the team on communicating with power. As he had already mentioned multiple times, any speaker must start out strong in order to garner the attention and support of the audience. Communicating with power breeds confidence and respect. There is a fine line between confidence and cockiness, and this fine line must be walked like a tightrope. Communicating with power requires practice and patience but can be one of the most effective business tools. Dalton reviewed some power movements that the team should consider:

- **Stance:** A wide stance with the feet apart indicates power. It is as simple as making yourself appear to be larger. Hands on the hips with the elbows out (termed the "Superman Stance") takes up space and indicates power.
- **Walk:** Walk with a quick pace and take long strides. Walking straight also, as previously mentioned, takes up more space and makes someone look bigger.

Dalton focused on these aspects and tried to customize his recommendations for each speaker. After the review of the videos and detailed discussion on each, the team discussed the videos candidly. Dalton's discussion seemed to open up the group to some constructive criticism. Everyone seemed enlightened by the feedback and results, with the exception of Rodger. Angela was smiling brightly and engaging with everyone and Austin was openly chatting, not waiting on others to start the conversation.

CHAPTER TEN

Thinking Quickly on Your Feet

D ALTON DISCUSSED LEADING practices in listening techniques and how to recall a person's name. He also discussed how the senior team could handle aggressive techniques with people. He introduced the STARS method for thinking quickly on your feet and how to use it effectively.

PEOPLE-CENTRIC SKILLS IN THIS CHAPTER

- Thinking Quickly on Your Feet
- Leading Practices in Listening Techniques
- How to Remember Names

KEY WORDS

- STARS Method for Quick Thinking
- Responding to Difficult Questions
- Remembering and Recall
- Listening Techniques

REMEMBERING NAMES

Dalton was fanatical about remembering names and details about people, especially clients. In his mind, this was one of the keys to his rapidly expanding business. "There is a massive difference between hearing and listening," he always says. "Hearing is a physical act that is natural and passive. Listening is a physical and mental process. It has to be active and learned. When people focus on listening rather than hearing, they will notice a significant change in all relationships, both personal and professional."

Dalton continued, "I have seen stats on the differences in speed of listening and thinking and there is a significant difference. We listen at 125 to 250 words per minute and think at 1,000 to 3,000 words per minute. In most cases, we listen when distracted or preoccupied, which also hinders listening."

People were always amazed at Dalton's ability to remember names and details. He would use these techniques throughout class and showcase them to see if people were able to see how he was able to remember so many things. In his mind, it was relatively easy.

"How do you become a better listener? It is simple: you try! Make an effort to listen! Do not play on your phone when someone else is talking. Use eye contact and listen to the words that are being utilized. Use active listening techniques to show the person you are speaking to that you are listening. Take a piece of what was just stated and use it in your follow-up statement." Some active listening techniques include:

- Using encouraging words and reassuring sounds to convey interest ("I see.")
- Restating in your own words what the person said
- Repeating exactly what the person said ("Mirroring")
- Reflecting to show you understand how they feel ("You seemed pretty upset by this.")
- Probing the interviewee's initial response in order to expand and/or clarify the information given ("Tell me more about that.")
- Summarizing ("These are the main ideas you stated.")

"Now, how do we remember names? Again, it is much easier than you might think. In this setting [Dalton was speaking to a group in attendance for training, so a classroom setting in this case], I will remember where people are seated and create a mental seating chart. You are not in that setting all the time so this is only a small piece of the equation. As you can see, every time I call on someone, I use their name. The first few times a person speaks in class, I ask them to use their name prior to speaking. Once you say a person's name three to five times, your ability to remember it increases significantly.

"If you are still not confident remembering names, there is nothing wrong with writing them down. I will write down new clients' names and little facts about them—kids, birthday, and so on. Anything to show the person you are talking to that you are listening and do care. Listening shows you care and that is a gamechanger."

ANSWERING QUESTIONS THAT SOUND LIKE AN ATTACK

Dalton discussed with the team some of the challenges they might face when presenting to a group. One that is always frustrating is the attendee who constantly wants to challenge or battle you or possibly hear themselves speak. At some point, someone might ask a question that could be viewed as a borderline attack. What is the appropriate way to respond?

- Don't confront the person. Don't say, "No, I think you're wrong." There are many ways to disagree with someone without saying, "You are wrong," or "I disagree." Almost immediately, their fight-or-flight instinct will kick in and they will become defensive.
- Affirm that their perspective is valid and appreciate the conversation. Do this by saying (try to avoid using the word "but"):
  - "That's an interesting point. Here's another way to look at it."
  - "I appreciate your thoughts. Let me give you a different perspective."
  - "I can see why you would have that opinion; here are my thoughts."

Everyone in the room will be interested to hear how you respond to the potential challenge. If you keep cool and say something positive before you deliver your retort, they will be impressed with your professionalism and your command of the situation.

Conflict management is one of Dalton's personal favorite topics and he loves to talk about it. Growing up with three brothers, he was not raised in a house that managed conflict well. Conflict was managed through fisticuffs until someone bled or one of their parents broke it up. Nowadays, he is well past that primal instinct but it is inside all of us.

Dalton loves to tell the story of his ex-wife and her primal instincts. Leslie is a little firecracker. She is a sweetheart but if she feels she or her family has been wronged, her primal instinct will rise up quickly. The specific incident that exemplifies how to handle conflict was between Leslie and her sister-in-law, Cori

(Dalton's brother's wife). Cori was very nice to people in person but would do things behind anyone's back to manipulate a situation in her favor. For years, Cori was always manipulating Dalton's mother to favor her over Leslie. Cori would do little subtle things that eventually drove Leslie crazy. One day, many years ago, Leslie finally told Dalton she had had enough and she was going to confront her. When Leslie confronts, she does so loudly and physically. Dalton asked her when she planned to have this well-thought-out and good-natured conversation (he could not turn off the sarcasm sometimes) and she said over the weekend when the entire family was going to get together at Dalton's parents' house. Instead of contradicting this plan (which would guide Leslie's anger toward him instead of Cori), he calmly sat down with her and said, "Honey, I know how frustrating it is to try to deal with Cori. You know my feelings about her. Do you think it is the best idea to have a potentially heated conversation with her in front of my parents, my brothers, and the 11 grandkids my parents have?"

Dalton said this without an ounce of sarcasm. Leslie broke down and cried a bit. She was immensely frustrated with Cori's constant backstabbing and manipulation. She was at her wit's end. Dalton, always in problem-solving mode, approached the conversation so that Leslie would be led to the answer, versus telling her the plausible solution.

Dalton continued, "In my opinion, Cori is behaving like this to elicit a very specific response from you. She wants you to behave in a way that makes you look bad and her look good. What do think is the reaction she is looking for?"

Leslie hated when Dalton did this. It was similar to being married to a different man; he would be nice, normal Dalton and then this guy would show up! She knew he was only trying to help, so she considered his question and continued the conversation.

Leslie sounded unsure when she answered, as if there was a question mark at the end of the sentence. "D, I think she wants me to get mad. She knows my personality and she knows I will eventually react emotionally. Is that what she is looking for?"

Dalton answered emphatically. "Yes, honey, that is *exactly* what she wants. She is not coming directly at you but you know she is always coming in hot. This is not subtracting two negative numbers; combatting negativity with negativity will not end positively!" Leslie rolled her eyes at this comparison but she also thought how well this would work in front of an audience.

Dalton continued, "Do the exact opposite of what she wants. Stay above her low-brow communication and when you see her this weekend, put on your brightest smile and be as warm as possible. Give her a big hug and ask her how her week was. Be as genuine as possible and let's kill this crazy woman with kindness." At first, Leslie *despised* this idea. She hated the thought of being warm and inviting to Cori. But after considering Dalton's plan, she thought it was a much better option than her original idea.

That weekend, Leslie did exactly what Dalton planned and it completely Cori caught offguard. Dalton saw surprise in her face and, after a few minutes of conversation where Leslie kept asking open-ended questions and utilized active listening to convey that she was engaged, Cori completely let her guard down. Fast forward many years later, and Liora and Cori's daughter Amber, who are cousins, are close friends. Dalton attributes the possibility of this relationship to Leslie's continued handling of Cori.

As shown in Leslie and Cori's story, answering hostile or aggressive questions with a matching response will simply make the whole process tense and will kill the overall atmosphere. On the other hand, if you respectfully answer an aggressive question by showing good grace and considering the question from a positive standpoint, you will disarm the hostile person and they potentially will back down from their confrontational position, whether through embarrassment for their unnecessary aggressiveness, or because they are impressed by your demeanor.

A few years back, Dalton created a very simple acronym to remember how to think on your feet in these types of situations:

STARS Method to Quick Thinking
- **S**top and Breathe
- **T**ake Time to Listen
- **A**sk to Repeat the Question
- **R**epeat the Question Yourself
- **S**ilence Can Be Deafening

Stop and Breathe
- In order for your voice to remain calm and for your brain to "think," you have to be as *relaxed* as possible.
- Take deep breaths (without being too obvious).
- Think positive.
- Clench invisible muscles (thighs, biceps, feet) for a few seconds and release.

Take Time to Listen
- Listening is the process of receiving, constructing meaning from, and responding to spoken and/or nonverbal messages, to hear something with thoughtful attention.

- Effective communication is two-way.
  - Dependent on speaking *and* listening.
  - Email *should be* one-way communication

Ask to Repeat the Question

- Does this make you look unsure?
  - It makes you look concerned that you want to give an appropriate response. It also gives the questioner an opportunity to rephrase and ask a question that is more on point. Another opportunity to assess the intentions of the questioner.
- If it is more specific or better worded, chances are the person really wants to learn more.
- If the repeated question is more aggressive than the first one, then you know the person is more interested in making you uncomfortable than anything else.

Repeat the Question Yourself

- Time to clarify exactly what is being asked.
- It also allows you to rephrase (*active listening*) if necessary and put a positive spin on the request.
- Ask for clarification.
- Narrow the focus.

Silence Can Be Deafening

- What does silence tell the speaker?
- It expertly communicates control (thoughts) and confidence in your answer.
- Rush to answer = Rush your words.
- It also tells the speaker that you might need more information.

CHAPTER ELEVEN

Coaching and Mentoring, Revisited

D ALTON COACHED AUSTIN and assists him in delivering feedback
to David Allison, a direct report he has struggled with since Austin's
promotion to vice president. Dalton helps Austin deliver delicate feedback to make sure he and David are aligned moving forward.

PEOPLE-CENTRIC SKILLS IN THIS CHAPTER

- What a Combined Coaching and Mentoring Approach Looks Like
- How to Deliver Contentious Feedback
- Use of Silence

KEY WORDS

- Coaching
- Mentoring
- Feedback
- Feedback Sandwich
- Constructive Criticism

At Kelli's request, Dalton hung around another evening so he could join Austin in chatting with David on Friday morning. He switched to a flight around lunch, which was aggressive, but he had to get home for the weekend. With the time change, Dalton would not be home until after 7:00 pm and it was his weekend with the kids. He hated traveling on Fridays, but he acquiesced to his clients—specifically Kelli. He liked Austin and wanted to be there to help and support him. In the back of his mind he also thought that if this went as well as anticipated, there should be plenty of add-on work as well. As an added bonus, the only seat he could move to on the new flight was already in first class. He traveled in first most of the time due to his status on American Airlines, but it was really nice not having to wait on an upgrade. He was Executive Platinum and was still trying to figure out how to get to Concierge Key.

He did not find out about this change until midday Thursday and had to make sure Leslie could keep the kids a little while longer. The kids were very disappointed but understood. Liora, being very mature and emotionally intelligent, handled this in stride. Caleb was also very mature in some ways but much more emotionally immature than his younger sister. Caleb struggled hearing this news but his dad promised he would be home for his game on Saturday and would hang out and watch a movie Saturday night, just the three of them. This seemed to calm him down. Dalton tried never to miss one of Caleb's games. Caleb wanted him there but Dalton got pure joy out of seeing his son excel and grow and it bothered him to miss any of his games as much as it bothered Caleb.

He did see this as an opportunity to see if Lauren wanted to hang out that evening for a bit. He really enjoyed her company and rarely spent time with someone that "got it." It was invigorating. Dalton sent her a casual text; he did not want to seem too forward but he really enjoyed spending time with someone with whom he had so much chemistry. "Hey—I am not leaving until tomorrow afternoon; want to grab a drink?"

Within a few minutes, she responded with an emphatic "Yes! Tell me when/where." Dalton was worn out from the long week, so he wanted to minimize his plans; they discussed meeting for happy hour after work at the bar at the Hilton where he was staying.

Dalton did not have time to change so he went directly to the hotel bar, ordered drinks for both of them, and scrolled through his phone, clearing as many emails as possible. Lauren casually walked in and warmly greeted Dalton. They continued their conversation from the previous two nights like it had never ended. Time flew by. Drinks, dinner, and more drinks. Dalton did bring up the subject of Angela and asked what her issues were going in with her. Lauren mentioned her frustrations and, after chatting with her, Dalton understood her issues in greater depth, even though she couldn't pinpoint them exactly. It was mainly due to her emotions and use of them. Dalton suggested that Lauren take a step back and try to understand rather than assume. Dalton said, "Angela is a single mom and without understanding her fully, I think it's shortsighted to think critically of her. With an open mind you might have a completely different perspective."

Before either looked up, it was closing in on 10:00 pm. Lauren had no interest in leaving; they were enjoying each other's company too much. Dalton invited Lauren up to his room to continue the evening but made it clear it was just to hang out and nothing more.

They retired upstairs and watched a movie; both fell asleep midway through, in each other's arms. Dalton's alarm went off at 5:30 am and Lauren hurriedly gathered her stuff and ran out, as she needed to get home and change. Before leaving, they hugged goodbye. This was not your friendly, casual hug. Lauren wrapped her arms around his neck and Dalton put his hands around her waist and slowly moved them to her back, gently rubbing her back while hugging her. The hug lasted much longer than either anticipated. Dalton walked her to the elevator and, before the elevator arrived at the 32nd floor to send Lauren downstairs to her car, she turned, came close to Dalton, moved him against the wall, and kissed him deeply. The elevator came and went and the kiss continued. Dalton eventually pulled away, not because he wanted to but because they both needed to.

After Lauren left, Dalton quickly packed and got dressed. He grabbed a quick breakfast and headed down to the office to meet Austin. He recounted the plan and was very interested to see how David would react to being confronted. He went through his notes and made sure Austin was on board with the plan to discuss with David:

- Discuss some of the rumors that Austin heard that make him think someone is trying to stir the pot, but he is moving forward with a clean slate.
- Austin understands David was very deserving of the position Austin was promoted to.
- That is not what happened so we are at a crossroads.
- What can Austin do to help David move past this?
- What are David's long-term goals at the company?
- Are there any projects David would like to be in charge of?
- How can Austin help him get there?
- Ask for David's assistance on creating a positive culture for the rest of the team.
- Give David the opportunity to elevate to Austin's official number two.

Dalton discussed with Austin the importance of the feedback sandwich when chatting with David. The environment needs to be viewed as positive, but Austin needs to make it clear that the previous behaviors would not be tolerated moving forward. Possibly that would not need to be said; it could very well be implied based on the situation. He walked through the feedback sandwich with Austin.

THE FEEDBACK SANDWICH

The Feedback Sandwich is a method of introducing feedback to any employee by surrounding it with praise. It starts with the bread (positive feedback) to begin the conversation on a high note. Be careful not to spend too much time praising at the beginning, because this will dilute the "meat" of the feedback message.

Next, deliver the opportunity for growth in a positive tone. Avoid accusations but remain focused on the message that must be delivered. The "meat" should be the most tangible part of the conversation. Finally, close the feedback session on a positive note. Praise a strength they have or, in this instance, tell them you are confident they are going to adjust and be successful. This balances out the constructive feedback with some positivity.

The feedback sandwich can be overused and Dalton made sure Austin knew he must be flexible with David. "If David reacts negatively to the start of the conversation, shift into the feedback quickly. Be flexible in your approach to this conversation. He might expect this and get frustrated when he hears the positive because he knows there is a lot of negative to come!" Austin understood and agreed with Dalton.

"It seems to be in vogue to rail on the feedback sandwich as people know it is coming; they want to hear the bad news right off the bat. As long as you are flexible in your approach to feedback, the sandwich concept still works very well!" Dalton exclaimed.

PROVIDING CONSTRUCTIVE CRITICISM

Dalton spent the few minutes before David came in to discuss a few key points on constructive criticism. Dalton explained that providing constructive criticism is a skill that requires you to focus on four key areas:

1. **Focus on one issue at a time.** Avoid addressing multiple issues. This will only cause confusion and frustration.

2. **Focus on timely, specific feedback.** Once you identify an issue, make sure you do not wait too long to deliver the critique. The more time passes, the less effective it will be.

3. Most important, **focus on observable actions or behaviors**. Avoid generalities.

4. Finally, **focus on a plan to change the behavior.** Depending on the extent of change that must happen, your plan may be a simple adjustment.

Dalton continued, "David's situation does not fit perfectly into these four key areas but, in general, these criteria fit in any situation."

Austin and Dalton walked over to the conference room where they were scheduled to meet David (Figure 11.1), a long room with an oblong table that seated 10. Dalton wanted to make sure they spaced out in the room so not to intimidate David. Physical spacing is important in any potential conflict.

Austin sat at the head of the table, the first seat as they walked in. Dalton sat behind the table, facing the door, in the middle seat. David walked in casually but with confidence. David and Dalton had never met, so they went through the normal pleasantries and Dalton wanted to ease David's concerns immediately. He stated, "Kelli has engaged me to assist some of the team in executive coaching and developing their coaching and mentoring. This seemed like

FIGURE 11.1 The conference room.

a great opportunity for me to meet some of Austin's management team." Based on David's reaction, he seemed passively apprehensive but accepting.

Austin commenced the dialogue. "David, I know you have a busy schedule and I appreciate you taking time to chat. I know we have not seen eye to eye on everything since I have taken this role. Starting today, I want us to have a clean slate. Everything in the past is in the past. I need help creating a culture of collaboration and cohesiveness. I cannot do this alone. Everybody respects your knowledge of the company and of IT. I want to create a department that we both can be proud of."

Austin was walking a fine line, complimenting David to build him up, but David already thought he should have Austin's job, so would this help or hinder collaboration? Dalton knew Austin was armed with specifics if David wanted to discuss the past but, hopefully, David saw the present that Austin was giving him: another chance, a clean slate.

David seemed to react well to this message. He sat tensely until Austin's initial message. He was very stiff and upright, sitting with his hands crossed on his chest and his legs crossed. After Austin's initial message, his shoulders relaxed, he uncrossed his legs and arms, and he leaned forward and took a deep breath.

"Austin, thank you," David began. "Anything I can do to help I would be happy to do." Both Austin and Dalton were somewhat surprised at how accepting David was of this message. Instead of responding immediately, neither gentleman said a word. Austin took a cue from Dalton and decided not to respond. David was peering down and avoiding eye contact for a few seconds. After approximately five seconds of silence, David, appearing contrite, continued, "I have not been happy over the past few months and it has probably shown. I have not been very supportive and, well, I hope we can move forward." Their use of silence showed David that more was expected in his response. Instead of filling the silence with words, they waited, and David filled the silence with additional necessary information. David's apology definitely felt sincere and Dalton knew this was a turning point for David and Austin. In Dalton's opinion, the conversation could have gone one of two ways: David accepted the message and made an effort to move forward and foster a positive environment (which appeared to be David's choice) or it could have gone downhill fast, with David in denial. Dalton was very happy with how this conversation was kicking off.

They continued the conversation for 20 more minutes, discussing next steps. David was not just participating, he was lending and generating ideas. Austin took a step back and listened to David's ideas and let him take the lead.

This was in line with the strategy they discussed prior to the meeting: empower your employees and give David the opportunity to shine as number two. If he does not like that position, then we will look at moving on without him. Thankfully, this does not appear to have been necessary.

Dalton walked back with Austin to his office, reviewing the conversation. Austin could not have been happier with the results. Dalton tempered his enthusiasm as David now had to follow through with results and that might be another story. Dalton recommended formal one-on-one meetings with David at least weekly to start to make sure David was receiving the appropriate amount of face-to-face conversation. Austin was very appreciative of Dalton's help and they discussed touching base in a few weeks to see how things were progressing.

12

Crisis Management

P RIOR TO CATCHING his flight, Dalton discussed the pros and cons of various ways to handle crisis management with Sojo CEO Brandon and CFO Kelli.

PEOPLE-CENTRIC SKILLS IN THIS CHAPTER

- What Is Crisis Management
- Potential Ways to Handle Crisis Management

KEY WORDS

- Crisis Management
- Transparent Communication

Dalton stopped by to say his goodbyes to Kelli. Kelli immediately brought him over to Brandon's office. He wanted to get Dalton's thoughts on how to handle the Julianne situation. They managed to catch Brandon in his corner office between meetings.

Brandon stood up to greet both of them, appearing cheerful and upbeat. The last few times Dalton had seen Brandon he was not so excited, so this was a pleasant change. "Dalton! Good to see you, my friend!" Brandon greeted Dalton warmly and sat back down. His body language was authoritative and confident. He leaned back in his executive chair, crossed his right leg over the left, and sat with his hands intertwined behind his head. Brandon began to speak. "I appreciate you stopping by. I know you have a flight to catch but I wanted to get your thoughts on next steps with Julianne. I don't think this will take more than a few minutes."

Brandon spent a few minutes filling Dalton in on where SoJo was at with Julianne. She had not admitted guilt but continued to use excuses and plausible deniability to push back on SoJo. With Dalton's assistance, SoJo's counsel felt comfortable that they could speak to law enforcement and prosecute at any time. No decision had been made. In fact, they had discussed with Julianne a mutual exit from the organization. Julianne would be required to pay back the funds in question but these were offset by the bonus she had earned and not yet received this year. It was decision time: should SoJo allow her to leave the organization, or should they hand this over to the authorities and pursue legal action? Brandon finalized the introduction with this: "Either way, this is coming to a conclusion, which is what I want. I know there is definitely a choice that is the easy way out, but I am not sure if it is the right answer for us."

Dalton went on a quick discursion; this was another of his favorite topics. "Brandon, you are correct. One of the routes to take is much easier than the other. Ultimately, it is up to you. I think you should consider which is the most risk-averse route. I'll add a side note with a quick story about Caleb and Liora. Both kids, in the span of a few months, had situations in school where something happened and their teacher told them they might call their parents about the issue. The issue itself was not important; the issue was whether the kids thought it was the right decision to tell us prior to their teacher calling, or whether they should not say anything, and risk their parents hearing it from the teacher first, and then try to explain why they did not tell them initially.

"Both Caleb and Liora told us before their teacher called, even though their teacher did not call. Why? My daughter gave me the best response. She said that everyone finds out about everything eventually, so I want to make sure you hear my side of the story first."

Brandon curled his lip and let out a slight "hmmm" as Dalton paused. He continued by giving two scenarios and suggesting that Brandon consider which would be more harmful:

- Coming out ahead of the message now, publicly (as much as possible) owning the message, and sending the right message to the public: we will not tolerate unethical behavior and our company is on the up-and-up.

OR

- Settling with Julianne and taking the chance on nothing getting out, but sending the wrong message internally and not transparently communicating internally, so the company became riddled with rumors and innuendo.

"Do we trust that Julianne will not be vengeful and fuel rumors? Do we trust that this will not get out publicly? If we do, then I think going the "'easy' route is viable. However, if we think there is a chance it gets out through the rumor mill, then SoJo could lose some credibility. There is a perception that many companies are gaining credibility by being transparent and getting ahead of the message."

Kelli and Brandon took in this information thoughtfully and Brandon chimed in, "Dalton, you have given us something to think about. Thanks for serving as a true consultant and not giving me a straight answer!" Dalton knew immediately he was saying this lightheartedly.

Dalton exited with pleasantries, gave Kelli a warm hug, and headed out to catch his Uber, rushing to catch his flight back to Dallas. He settled in on the flight, excited to be heading home. Dalton did not like the travel but he was used it. It was always exciting to come home—to see the kids, for the weekend, for the time to take a proverbial deep breath, for all of the above!

As everyone boarded, Dalton received a text from Lauren, raw and sweet: "Enjoyed your training and spending some time with you. Would love to see you again soon. XOXO." The text made him smile cheek to cheek. He thought about the possibilities as he zoned out and the flight took off for Dallas on a beautiful fall afternoon.

Epilogue

D ALTON HURRIEDLY DROPPED the kids off at school and rushed downtown. The man who is always busy had been even busier than normal. Baxter connected Dalton with his publisher and Dalton published his first fictional business novel, loosely based on his own personal experience. It was a labor of love and very time-consuming but he was very proud of the final product. In fact, sales in the first month of publication had been higher than expectations, and with the work of his agent, Dalton was about to make his television debut with an interview on a local morning show. He loved speaking in front of groups but television was a whole new ballgame. He was extremely nervous, yet—as he mentioned to the kids all the time—if you are nervous, it just means what you are doing is important, so have fun with it. This made him smile.

The kids enjoyed the concept of writing a book so much that they were working with their dad on a book on communication skills for kids; they even thought of a catchy name (Kid-Centric Skills). They planned on publishing it sometime over the summer. Business and life continue to clash but Dalton is continually working on better balance.

Normalcy for the kids was helped by Leslie getting settled into her own routine after the divorce. She was dating a nice, religious, older gentleman who was more her speed. The kids seemed to like him or at least tolerate him, which was a step in the right direction. Dalton and Lauren saw each other once a month and she had met the kids a few months ago. The kids liked her spunkiness and energy. The two still dated other people but were both just filling time until they could see each other again.

Dalton continued to work with Kelli and her team and expanded their work throughout the organization. With SoJo's new technology, the company was rapidly expanding and Dalton and his team were being used in multiple ways.

Brandon and the board of directors weighed their options with Julianne and chose to pursue charges against her. The company initially took a small hit to their reputation but their handling of this situation was publicly lauded and, internally, it helped strengthen the culture immensely.

As Dalton pulled into the parking lot of WFEA-TV near the American Airlines Center (where the Mavericks play), he thought of a client meeting he had scheduled that afternoon with Barry at DCL Technologies. He was meeting to discuss how to continue to assist in their change management efforts. He thought through how most people loved their routines and hated change. Dalton did not mind routine, but there was nothing too routine about his life anymore. That thought made him grin at the irony; he was assisting DCL with change management and his life, normalcy was change.

Appendix

EMOTIONAL INTELLIGENCE SELF-ASSESSMENT

Question	Strongly Agree	Agree	Disagree	Strongly Disagree
I usually stay composed, positive, and unflappable even in trying moments.				
I can think clearly and stay focused on the task at hand under pressure.				
I'm organized and careful in my work.				
I regularly seek out fresh ideas from a wide variety of sources.				
I'm good at generating new ideas.				
I can smoothly handle multiple demands and changing priorities.				
I'm results-oriented, with a strong drive to meet my objectives.				
I like to set challenging goals and take calculated risks to reach them.				
I'm always trying to learn how to improve my performance, including asking younger people for advice.				
I readily make sacrifices to meet an important organizational goal.				
I am able to admit my own mistakes.				
I usually or always meet commitments and keep promises.				
I hold myself to my goals.				

The company's mission is something I understand and can identify with.				
The values of my team influence my decisions and clarify the choices I make.				
I actively seek out opportunities to further the overall goals of the organization and enlist others to help me.				
I pursue goals beyond what's required or expected of me in my current job.				
Obstacles and setbacks may delay me a little, but they don't stop me.				
Cutting through red tape and bending outdated rules are sometimes necessary.				
I seek fresh perspectives, even if that means trying something totally new.				
My impulses or distressing emotions don't often get the best of me at work.				
I can change tactics quickly when circumstances change.				
Pursuing new information is my best bet for cutting down on uncertainty and finding ways to do things better.				
I usually don't attribute setbacks to a personal flaw (mine or someone else's).				
I operate from an expectation of success rather than a fear of failure.				
TOTAL (PER COLUMN)				
MULTIPLY TOTAL COLUMN BY:	4	3	2	1
SUBTOTAL				
OVERALL EMOTIONAL INTELLIGENCE SCORE				

SCORES:	
You are strongly functioning in emotional intelligence; you are highly motivated, good in high-pressure situations and can read and acknowledge yours and other people's emotions and focus these emotions on productive means.	85 or above
No significant issues; you are functioning well in emotional intelligence but could improve to optimize EI's uses.	70-84
Potential issues exist; EI can be improved with practice and acknowledgment of areas of concern.	50-69
A significant reassessment in the key areas of emotional intelligence is necessary.	Below 50

 ## CHAPTER 2: PEOPLE-CENTRIC SKILLS

Nine Facial Indicators Providing Reliable Clues:

- **Micro-Expressions:** Involuntary expressions that briefly flash across the subject's face.
- **Squelched Expressions:** Indicates that a liar is trying to hide emotions, but in contrast to a micro-expression, a squelched expression is performed on purpose and involves the signaling of multiple emotions.
- **Reliable Muscle Patterns**: Reliable muscles are not easy to control. These include the eye muscle that narrows the eyelids, the orbicularis oculi that produces crow's feet lines at the outer corners of the eye. The orbicularis oculi is difficult to move into a smile when your emotional state does not support smiling. We must carefully watch the entire face for clues of deception. When someone is attempting to deceive, their true emotions and thoughts are often displayed via the reliable muscle patterns on the upper portion of the face (forehead, eyebrows, eyes).
- **Blink Rates**: Blinking can be voluntary or involuntary, but deception can trigger higher rates of blinking.
- **Pupil Dilation:** Pupil dilation is a reliable indicator of emotion. We are not aware of anyone who can control the size of their pupils. Unusually dilated pupils are generally associated with fear but can also be caused by other uncontrolled emotions.
- **Tears:** While tears are obvious indicators of distress, they are not hard to fake. Take note of tears, but do not be misled by them.

- **Asymmetrical Expressions:** Genuine emotion, apart from contempt, is displayed on both sides of the face. Attempts to conceal emotion or portray a particular emotion are often limited to one side of a person's face.
- **Timing:** True emotion is expressed spontaneously. The timing difference for feigned emotion is brief, but it is there if you watch for it.
- **Duration:** Genuine emotion generally lasts between 5 and 10 seconds. A fixed expression held beyond 10 seconds may indicate that the subject is attempting to hide their true thoughts and feelings."[1]

Differences between Fraud Interviews and Audit or Other Types of Interviews

Internal Audit Interview	Fraud Investigation Interview
Objective: To gain an understanding	Objective: To obtain information regarding involvement or noninvolvement
■ Friendly conversational format	■ Friendly and conversational format to obtain a baseline and establish rapport
■ Designed to obtain information and build/retain the client relationship	■ Open-ended questions used to obtain/assess facts
■ Tone and wording crafted to get audit client to relax	■ Yes/No questions used to assess behavior
■ Questions focus on gaining an understanding of a process, journal entry or accounting rationale	■ **BASIC** Framework/methodology
■ Open-ended questions used to collect facts	■ **B**aseline behavior (laughter, movement, tone, pitch, reaction times, and expressions)
	■ **A**sk open-ended questions
	■ **S**tudy the clusters
	■ **I**ntuit the gaps; if something doesn't add up, ask more questions
	■ **C**onfirm[2]

 ## PLAUSIBLE DENIABILITY

Plausible deniability is defined as the ability of people to deny knowledge of or responsibility for any damnable actions committed by others in an organizational hierarchy because of a lack of evidence that can confirm their participation, even if they were personally involved in or at least willfully ignorant of the actions. The lack of evidence to the contrary ostensibly makes

[1] Meyer, P. (2010). *Liespotting: Proven Techniques for Detecting Deception.* New York: St. Martin's Press.
[2] Ibid.

the denial plausible—that is, credible—although sometimes it merely makes it unactionable. The term typically implies forethought, such as intentionally setting up the conditions to plausibly avoid responsibility for one's (future) actions or knowledge.[3]

When interviewing, it is important to listen intently for plausible deniability. Specifically, when the question asked is a closed-ended question (most likely a yes/no answer), and the person gives something other than the requisite answers:

- "Most of the time, that occurs."
- "I believe so."
- "When I am doing it, that is the way it is done."
- "I am pretty sure that is what occurs."

This gives the speaker an "out"; they have answered the question (in their mind) truthfully but answered it deliberately. It does not mean the person is lying; in their opinion, the question has more than one possible answer. The interviewer must listen, catch, and follow up on questions answered in this manner. When questions are answered with plausible deniability, the interviewer should ask follow-ups such as:

- Why do you say, "Most of the time?"
- "Are there other ways this can be processed?"
- "Are there different ways it could be processed, such as someone else processing it?"

 ## CHAPTER 3: PEOPLE-CENTRIC SKILLS

Emotional Intelligence

Emotional intelligence is a set of skills demonstrating the ability an individual has to recognize their behaviors, moods, and impulses, and to manage them best according to each unique situation.

Understanding the causes of emotions and how to use them to your advantage can help you to identify who you are and how you interact best with others.

---

[3] https://en.wikipedia.org/wiki/Plausible_deniability

EQ Self-Appraisal

- **Self-Management:** Control of emotions, impulses, and adapting to changing circumstances
- **Self-Awareness:** Awareness of one's emotions and recognizing their impact while using intuition to guide decisions
- **Empathy:** Ability to sense, understand, and react to others' emotions while comprehending social networks
- **Self-Motivation:** Staying focused in all critical situations; minimal dependency on others to motivate

Self-Management

Consistency: Stability/Consistency is key to self-management. If you're always changing, this can cause others to question your beliefs and what you stand for and can also cause you to become confused about what you truly believe.

Stick to the Plan: Do it right and do it in a timely way. Plans are made for a reason. Stick to them but be flexible as necessary. The goal is set; it must be met.

Be Accountable: Things do not always work out as planned. That is normal—probably more normal than working out. You have to be able to admit that and then use your flexibility to get things back on track. Flexibility is key; do not worry about it—move forward.

Educate Yourself: Once we stop learning, we stop living. Do not let change pass you by; embrace it. Read, read, and read some more. Talk and listen to mentors and peers; look for different perspectives. Once we stop evolving, we will be behind the times.

Stay Mentally and Physically Fit: This is a very important part of being able to practice the other aspects of self-management. Exercising your body is just as crucial to self-management as exercising your mind. A body that is not well rested, nutritionally fed, or physically exercised can lead to emotional and physical illnesses.

Self-Awareness

- Ability to perceive one's skills and knowledge accurately and realistically
- This is the first step to the process of full acceptance or change

- Unless someone understands why they think or act the way they do, they will never fully appreciate themselves or see the importance of making changes to improve.
- Gives power and a sense of peace/happiness

A lack of self-awareness prevents you from realizing your worth in the company or even the quality of the work you perform. This can have a serious impact on your personal and professional life. Not only will you have doubts about yourself, but the people you lead will also begin to question your competence, which could ultimately lead to a lack of leadership effectiveness.

Self-Regulation

- Ability to control one's emotions, desires, and behaviors in order to reach a positive outcome
- There is an art to finding the balance between expressing one's feelings and avoiding unnecessary tension

Direct reflection of the type of pressure one is experiencing. There is good and bad pressure:

1. **Good:** Result of an assertive but nonharmful atmosphere. A person views the people around them as an inspiration and uses this as motivation, which can lead to the acquisition of self-regulation.
2. **Bad:** When the atmosphere is critical and harmful, this pressure does not motivate and self-regulation is lost.

Use Emotions to Facilitate Thinking

- How one feels will determine how he or she views situations.
- This is also key when interpreting communications.
- Emotions can overwhelm commonsense.
- Negative conflict is often driven by a lack of logical thinking.
- If emotions cloud thinking, it is very difficult to think straight and make sound decisions.
  - Having control of your emotion and understanding when they cloud your judgment leads to clearer thinking and more sound decision making.

Gaining Control

- Control over yourself, your thoughts, and emotions is one of the most important aspects of emotional intelligence.
- Having control or the lack thereof could be the difference between building or destroying a successful career.

Using Coping Thoughts

When a situation arises that requires coping skills, try the following:

- **Take a deep breath.** Deep breathing has an amazingly calming effect on the brain. By doing so, one can easily avoid the first, natural reaction to a stressful situation. This is key because the first reaction is usually an emotional, potentially irrational, and illogical reaction.
- **Step away.** Mentally take yourself away from the situation and analyze the issue itself. Analyze the issue without emotion. This is easy to say and much harder to do. Ask the following questions:
  - Does this really matter?
  - Does it matter now?
  - Will it matter tomorrow? One month? Ever?
  - Does it truly impact you?
  - Am I allowing my emotions to override my rational thinking?
- **Use positive thinking.** Do not approach any situation with thoughts of anger, sadness, or other negative emotions. Think happy thoughts. This does not allow you to avoid the problem, but rather is a way to prepare you to tackle it in a productive manner. Every problem has a potential solution.

Understand Emotions and How to Manage Them in the Workplace

- Understanding one's emotions and learning how to use them is the responsibility of each person.
- Can we ignore them? *No.* Emotions are part of all of us and need to be used, understood, and controlled appropriately.

Example: You are a manager and your team is about to miss an important deadline. You can decide if you should stress and what level you should stress to in terms of how necessary it is for you to meet the deadline. There are numerous options, so you have to decide which makes sense for you and the team:

- Call a team meeting and explain the ramifications of not meeting the deadline.
- Yell and scream and tell the team we have to meet the deadline no matter what.
- Make a mandatory 24/7 workday to meet the deadline.
- Don't worry about the deadline and let it play out.

This would also be a good time to listen to team members to find out if there is something out of their control that is preventing them from doing their job.

The first option seems to be the most rational. A less calm and more volatile method would be to yell at everyone and tell them to get to work. Deciding which style is best can be done by weighing the pros and cons of each, as well as which would result in the most positive outcome. Do not rely solely on how you feel, but also on what makes logical sense.

Role of Emotional Intelligence at Work

Emotional intelligence plays a vital role in the workplace. How people feel about themselves, interact with others, and handle conflict is directly reflected in the quality of work produced. The more confident and "bought in" employees are, the better the work product produced. Social proficiencies are developed as a result of emotional intelligence.

Social Proficiencies

Empathy: Being aware of others' feelings and exhibiting compassion. Truly making an effort to understand why someone feels the way they do.

Intuition: An inner sense of the feelings of others. Understanding others without asking about others. A general feel of how another is based on nonverbal cues.

Political Acumen: The ability to communicate with a strong business influence including leadership skills and conflict resolution.

Disagreeing Constructively

- Means to do so in a positive, productive manner.
- The purpose is not to argue to get your point across.
- This is not used to be negative or destructive of other's thoughts.
- Workplace disagreement is a common occurrence.
- Companies look for the most effective ways to carry out operations and therefore invest in process improvement strategies, which opens the floor for discussion and compromise.
- Constructive disagreement acknowledges and confirms another's ideas before presenting your own.

 ## CHAPTER 5: PEOPLE-CENTRIC SKILLS

Mode of Communication

Choosing the right mode of communication drives productive communication. When picking the right mode, regardless of what is communicated, it will be communicated effectively. If the wrong mode is chosen, there is an increased chance of confrontation, regardless of how simplistic the message is. (See Figure 5.1 in chapter 5.)

In general, the main modes of communication are:

- In Person
- Phone
- Email
- Text/Instant Message

The mode of communication selected should be based on specific communication criteria:

- **Emotion:** Direct correlation between the level of emotion driven by the communication and the more personal nature of the mode of communication (inperson)
- **Urgency:** Indirect correlation between the speed of communication and the personal nature of the communication
- **Dialogue:** Direct correlation between the level of discussion/dialogue necessary and the more personal nature of the mode of communication (in person/by phone)

CHAPTER 6: PEOPLE-CENTRIC SKILLS

Change Management

Change Management: Initial Strategy

Strategy Component	Company-Specific Message Example
Description of the proposed change vision, and its goals	Evolve the business processes, technology, and culture at DCL as we continue to grow over the next five years.
The reasons(s) why the change is necessary	We expect significant growth over this time. We must evolve the organization or face significant disruption in our strategy and ability to recruit top personnel.
Critical success measures and key performance indicators	<ul><li>Project needs for business processes, technology and culture for the next five-plus years</li><li>Perform gap analysis for each</li><li>Determine critical needs for each</li><li>Change management team to track progress for each</li></ul>
Project stakeholders and stakeholder groups and their involvement	<ul><li>Senior management</li><li>Change champions</li><li>Everyone!</li></ul>
Key messages to communicate	See above.

Five Natural Reactions to Change

- **Denial:** May be reluctant to listen or may deny any facts or information presented to support the change if they are not informed in a timely way or are told after the fact.
- **Resistance:** Common reaction stems from fear of the unknown.
- **Anger:** When change occurs and the norm is disturbed, people can experience anger. They may lash out and become uncooperative during this time.
- **Indifference:** People just may not care, or the change may not have an impact on their routines or work. Be wary of this; the change may be intended to have an impact, but if the individual is indifferent about the change, they may not understand or accept it.
- **Acceptance:** Changes occur for the better and have a positive influence on those involved. Even with positive change, acceptance may not happen right away but should occur more quickly, as opposed to when the change is perceived to be negative.

Integral Steps to Help Employees and Leaders Become More Resilient

1. Have a Realistic Picture of What Your Capabilities Are but Do Not Limit Yourself
   a. Realism is the key to growth. However, realism should not be a limitation.
2. Have No Fear of Failure; Embrace Failure as a Learning Opportunity
   a. The world today is full or participation trophies.
   b. Losing = Learning
   c. Every Great Leader Has Failed!
3. Embrace Risk-Taking
   a. Inherent in every risk is an opportunity.
4. Focus on Continuing to Develop Critical Thinking Skills (Think Outside the Box)
   a. Focus on new approaches for everything.
   b. Continue to reinvent yourself.
   c. Suspend immediate judgment if you are in the middle of a change.
5. Embrace Detailed, Regimented Project Management throughout the Organization
   a. Use a planner or planning software to keep to-do lists, track plans, commitments, and next steps for each change initiative.
   b. Break down complex or ambiguous situations into manageable chunks.
   c. Find a coach who has strong organizational skills.
6. Maintain Focus on Long-Term Goals and Objectives but Be Flexible
   a. Reassess goals and objectives periodically.

 ## CHAPTER 7: PEOPLE-CENTRIC SKILLS

> "The goal of communication is not merely to communicate a message. The goal of communication is to gain acceptance and understanding of the message."
>
> —Danny M. Goldberg

Building Rapport

The key to relationship-building is:

- **Smile and look approachable.** As he taught in class, the power of a true smile is contagious and intoxicating.
- **Ask open-ended questions.** Open-ended questions are, in essence, not questions at all, but more so request statements. Instead of asking, "What do you do?" Dalton would ask, "Tell me about your work or your passion; hopefully they are the same." These types of questions elicit a much more detailed response.
- **70/30 Rule.** Dalton actively changed this to the 90/10 rule. He was paid to speak. He *loved* to speak. He also knew that he always had plenty of opportunities to speak. Not everyone else did. Every person wants to be heard. Dalton had experienced the phenomenon of being a great listener. Not only does the person you are talking to think you are a great listener, but they really view you as a great conversationalist, and you have barely said anything!
  - Personalize interactions and look for common themes to bond over.
  - Use eye contact and active listening to show you care.
  - Let the other person lead the conversation. Let them take it where they want.

Five Language Registers/Styles

Each level can have an appropriate use that is determined by varying situations. The proper language register depends on the audience (who), the topic (what), purpose (why) and location (where). The five language registers are:

1. **Static Register:** This style *rarely* changes. It is "frozen" in time and content (e.g. the Pledge of Allegiance, laws).
2. **Formal Register:** This style is used in formal settings and is a one-way communication. This use of language usually follows a commonly accepted format. It is generally impersonal and formal (e.g. sermons, speeches, announcements).
3. **Consultative Register:** This is the standard form of communication. People engage in a mutually accepted structure of communications. This form is professional and in line with societal expectations (e.g. when strangers meet, communications between an employee and supervisor, doctor and patient).

4. **Casual Register:** This is informal language used by peers and friends. Slang and colloquialisms are normal. Casual is "group" language. Texting can also be viewed as casual.

5. **Intimate Register:** This communication is private. It is reserved for close family members or intimate people (e.g. spouses, significant others, siblings, parents and children).[4]

People can usually transition from one language register to an adjacent one without encountering any major issues. Skipping one or more levels is confusing, to say the least.

Body Language: Gesture Cluster

Note: This is also discussed in more detail in chapter 9.

Interest/Attentive

- Upright posture or leaning in toward the person speaking when focusing or when very interested in what is said
- Legs and body facing the person speaking
- Hands (when leaning forward) on the table directly in front of the person, connected or taking notes
- Legs crossed but minimal movement
- Head slightly turns when considering what is said

Boredom/Defensive/Lack of Interest

- Leaning back in chair
- Arms crossed or hands connected behind head
- Leg swinging or kicking when crossed
- No eye contact
- Constant eye rolling
- Low sound effects (blowing air, sighing, etc.)

Surprise/Frustration:

- Eyebrows initially raised
- Head moves backward as the question is asked, literally taken aback by the question
- Eyebrows furrowing as head moves forward

---

[4] Montano-Harmon, M.R. "Developing English for Academic Purposes" California State University, Fullerton.

- Nostrils flaring before answering the question
- Arms in front of the body (crossed)

Neurolinguistic Programming

In general, a person's eyes tend to look in a specific direction when someone is recalling information (to their left) or constructing information (to their right). The six quadrants are as follows:

- **Visually Constructed:** Constructing a site mentally (making up a story)
- **Visually Remembered:** Remembering something that has occurred (seen)
- **Audio Constructed:** Creating a sound or imagining what something sounds like
- **Audio Remembered:** Recalling what a certain voice sounds like or another sound
- **Feeling/Kinesthetic:** Remembering how something smelled, tasted, or a specific feeling
- **Auditory Digital/Internal Dialog:** When someone might talk to themselves, some type of internal dialog[5]

Presentation Preparation

Identifying the Audience

- Who is the audience?
- What do you know about them?
- Do they care about the topic?
- Should they care about the topic?
- What's important to them?
- Do they have any misconceptions about your topic?
- Could there be a lack of understanding?
- Can you predict the questions they might have?

Audience Profile/Questionnaire

- **Education:** Regardless of education and savviness, try speaking to a level anyone can comprehend. If the audience is well-versed in the topic, a higher level can definitely be used.

---

[5] https://www.nlpworld.co.uk/nlp-glossary/e/eye-accessing-cues/

- **Familiarity with Topic:** What do people know about the topic already and what do you need to explain? Is this a controversial topic?
- **Audience:** Who in the audience do we need on our side? Who is the pulse-setter of the group? Is this presentation to convince the group of something or to mediate an issue between groups?
- **Interest in the Topic:** Do they care about the topic? What do people care about? Is this topic important to them? What's important to them?
- **Possible Misconceptions:** Which incorrect ideas might you need to correct? In most cases, this should be addressed at the beginning of the presentation. Until this is addressed, the audience will be confused and their guard will be up.
- **Attitude:** Are people hostile, supportive, curious, worried? The attitude of your audience will affect the tone of your speech. The time of day and day of week will also potentially impact the attitude.

Keys to Public Speaking

- The mood and opinion of any audience is important. It will influence the tone and content of the speech; a nervous or concerned audience will require an element of comfort or reassurance, while an excited audience will want to share a positive, electric atmosphere.
- Speakers will lose their audience quickly if they go over their time allotment.
- Do not discount the importance of smiling when presenting.
- Engaging an audience will make everyone pay attention more intently. Hearing one voice consistently for a period of time is more challenging to pay attention to than hearing numerous voices and banter over the same period of time and on the same topic.
- When emphasizing a point, move closer to the group.
- Alter voice inflection when necessary and to reiterate key points.
- Do not end with a Q&A (Questions and Answers) sessions.
    - If you end with Q&A, you might lose control of your message.
    - As a presenter, you want your message to be flexible, but you also want to control the message.
    - Prior to your final slide/message, pause and ask for any final questions or comments.
    - Final Slide: Summarize the three key messages you want everyone to leave the room with.

CHAPTER 8: PEOPLE-CENTRIC SKILLS

Coaching: A coach tends to specialize in improving one or two areas of development at a time, laser-focus on those areas and progressively moves to other areas of focus as needed. In general, a coach tutors/instructs/motivates a person to achieve a specific goal or skill. Their interaction is planned and structured.

Mentoring: Mentoring happens for a varied purpose or goal. Varied purpose and goal. A mentor is a trusted counselor or guide.[6] Mentoring is supporting someone's path of learning. Fundamentally, mentoring the role of a teacher. Mentoring can include coaching however, it is different from coaching.

Difference: Mentorship is more voluntary in nature and less formal. The mentor and protégé focus on a broad development goal. Mentoring can encompass many complex areas of development.

Effective coaching has to be done in a trusting environment. There is no alternative to this. Trust is the foundation of all strong personal and professional relationships.

Avoid using the coach session as a venue to deliver reprimands and bad news. This is not the place for that kind of information. Avoid using coaching when only negative things need to be addressed. Coaching should be a purposeful event that happens regularly and is void of negative information. This is not to say you cannot discuss specific performance issues after the initial session. It just has to be presented in a way that speaks more to development than to punishment. Without trust, you will not be able to coach well.

Some of the benefits realized when combining coaching with mentorship include:

- Increased flexibility
- Supervise while acting autonomously
- Empowers employees to decide whether they want to continue to be successful in this environment or take a different path
- Employees are empowered in the path they take
- Enlist the assistance of other managers in the management of employees as necessary

---

[6] https://www.merriam-webster.com/dictionary/mentor

Building Trust

1. **Maintain positive body language:**
   a. Open gestures tell the other person you are approachable and open to communication. Open hand gestures show you are drawing team member's ideas in and will help them know you are paying attention.
   b. Good posture will show you are standing at attention and interested. A healthy social distance of 6 feet will usually cue you're listening intently. Do not impede on their personal space as they may feel intimidated.
   c. Open posture will show the other person you are open to feedback and moving the conversation forward.
   d. When delivering constructive feedback, lean away from the person to which you are delivering the feedback. Consider leaning toward an angle and lesson eye contact so the person can absorb the feedback without someone gazing at them. If you lean back, this will lessen the blow and come off as less aggressive.
   e. By leaning your head to the side after delivering feedback, it shows interest in their response and empathy for their response.
2. **Employ the 70/30 rule:** Listening gives the other person a voice. Having a voice helps to build trust. Focused, active listening is key.
3. **Always respect your team members:** Respect is foundational to trust.
4. **Keep things confidential:** If they do not feel they can tell you anything, they will never open up. If you cannot keep the information being presented confidential, then you must state that ahead of time.
5. **Keep your promises:** Broken promises equate to broken trust. When you say, "You have my word," you should mean it.
6. **Be honest and transparent:** Provide candid, tactfully direct feedback, and be as transparent as possible. Transparency builds trust.
7. **Tell them you believe in them:** For an employee to trust their supervisor, they need to know they are supported. By telling them you believe in them, trust is built.

 CHAPTER 9: PEOPLE-CENTRIC SKILLS

Organizing the Presentation

Using an outline, these essential parts of a presentation should be considered:

- **Opening:** Some speakers like to begin a presentation with a joke to put the audience at ease. Other ways to start include asking a rhetorical question, giving people a surprising statistic, or telling a brief anecdote that is related to the topic.

- **Body:** The body contains your supporting arguments for the key points introduced in the opening.
- **Review:** Restate the key points briefly for those who may have tuned out.
- **Closing:** Restate the main point of your presentation. In some cases, you may want to give people a "call to action."

Creating a Presentation

- If you feel writing out part of your speech is necessary, the best thing to do is create an elevator pitch for your speech.
- Be flexible!
  - Things go wrong; stuff is bound to happen. How you handle adversity shows people who you truly are.
  - People get flustered when bad things happen and the audience picks up on the negative emotion quickly and can form a negative impression of the speaker. Artful speakers treat unexpected problems humorously to put everyone at ease and build a rapport with the audience.
- Often, it is enough simply to know that you may encounter such problems and to have an attitude that technical difficulties come and go.

Being Prepared

Preparedness is key to mastering any skill. Practice makes perfect, however, there is such a thing as being overprepared. Being prepared serves many purposes. It gives you the self-confidence to get up in front of many people.

Checking Out the Venue

Some things to look for include:

- Is there room to walk around throughout the presentation?
- Is there a podium?
- Is there a raised stage?
- What equipment is available?

Overcoming Nervousness and Preparing Mentally: Before the Presentation

Nervousness causes adrenaline to be released into the blood, sending impulses to organs to create a specific response.[7] Adrenaline causes a noticeable increase in strength and performance, in addition to heightened awareness during stress.[8] Too much adrenaline can be damaging, but nerves are natural.

Channel your nervousness by forcing yourself to speak clearly and to make eye contact with your listeners. Like any professional athlete preparing for a big game, you need to keep yourself in a positive frame of mind as you prepare for your own big event:

- **Exercise.** If you enjoy physical or mental exercise, stay in your routine and do it the night before or that morning.
- **Eat Right.** Eating healthy is key to continuing to build your self-confidence. Not only that, certain foods can make you feel lethargic.
- **Sleep.** A good night of rest helps to combat nerves.
- **Hydration.** Dry mouth can happen to any speaker. Staying hydrated by having water will help to combat dry mouth. Drinks with caffeine will exacerbate the problem.
- **Chew Gum.** Jaw movement can help release nervous energy. Research has shown an increased vigilance, a lower level of anxiety, a decrease in the experience of stress, and a lower elevation of cortisol levels when people chew gum.[9]

Overcoming Nervousness and Preparing Mentally: During the Presentation

- **Breathe**. Progressive breathing before, during, and even after your presentation is key. When you breathe deeply, it sends a message to your brain to calm down and relax.[10] The brain then passes this message on to the body. Indicators of stress (increased heart rate, high blood pressure, etc.) all decrease when you breathe deeply.[11]

---

[7] https://www.hormone.org/your-health-and-hormones/glands-and-hormones-a-to-z/hormones/adrenaline
[8] https://www.hormone.org/your-health-and-hormones/glands-and-hormones-a-to-z/hormones/adrenaline
[9] https://www.skillsyouneed.com/present/presentation-nerves.html
[10] https://www.uofmhealth.org/health-library/uz2255
[11] https://www.uofmhealth.org/health-library/uz2255

- **Slow Down/Pause**. Nerves tend to make everyone speak faster. Appropriately pause to emphasize a key point or repeat it. This give the audience a moment to absorb the message.
- **Movement.** Moving around throughout a presentation will help use some nervous energy. There are numerous benefits of movement during a presentation, however, this is primarily from the perspective of managing nerves.

Appearing Confident in Front of the Crowd

Someone who exudes confidence demonstrates specific characteristics:

- No notes or notecards (in hands). Notes are used as a crutch, and as previously mentioned, speakers often forget about the notes.
- Being well-organized can also improve your self-confidence.
- Smiling is a surefire way to gain engagement and lessen nerves.

The most important thing to remember in order to deliver a confident presentation is awareness of your surroundings.

Delivering Your Speech

Ways to make sure your presentation begins on the right tone:

- Start strong by preparing an opening that will capture the audience's attention.
- Check the volume of your voice. A powerful, friendly voice will garner the audience's attention immediately.
- Smile. Smiling is one of the key aspects to engaging people and eliciting questions and feedback.

The opening should be very brief; in most cases one to two minutes. In that short timespan, you need to present yourself and your topic in a way that will make your audience want to pay attention to you. A few different ways to approach this include:

- **Traditional**. Start with one to two minutes on the topic at hand. Introduce the topic and the key supporting points that will reiterate the topic.

- **Questioning.** Start with a question related to the topic so that, based on their answers and discussion, the group is naturally lead back to the key topic.
- **Dialogue.** Similar to questioning, start with a discussion, not necessarily a question.
- **Controversial.** This approach is a little trickier and not necessarily for a novice speaker. Start with a statement that is the opposite of your main topic to engage the audience. For example, try opening with a statement along the lines of "Here is something that I do not theoretically believe is necessary." Follow this up by saying, "You may not agree with me but give me a chance to prove this to you here and now."

How to Lose an Audience in the First Two Minutes

- Stand behind the podium the beginning of the presentation.
- Start with a whimper.
- Tell the audience you are new at this.
- Tell the audience this not your best topic.
- Do not smile.
- Do not command the audience.

Flexibility Is Key!

Audiences can lose interest for many reasons. some ways to reengage them include:

- Ask questions. Knowing attendee names is also key to engagement.
- Have a member of the audience come to the front of the room to help you with a demonstration. Having people get involved is a great way to reengage.
- Conduct a straw poll and take opinions from both sides to start a discussion.
- Introduce a brief, exciting digression (go off-topic for two or three minutes). Make sure the story correlates at least a little to the topic at hand. People enjoy this personal approach, especially when the topic might be a little dry and this livens it up a bit.
- Use a brief anecdote (preferably one that has something to do with your topic). Use personal experiences but be able to wind back to the key topic.

Reading Body Language

Head

Head Positioning The position of a person's head can be a surefire and easy-to-read indicator of emotion. Some key considerations include the following:

Movement and Position
- **Nodding:** Nodding typically indicates agreement with what has been said. The speed of the nod can have varying meanings. Faster could signal impatience, gentler could mean appreciation and interest, and slow can be a sign of interest or a polite, fake signal. Look to other eyes for confirmation.
- **Head Firm/Head Up:** Person is listening with an open mind and without bias.
- **Head Down:** Opposite of head up, as this position indicates disinterest or rejection for what is said (possibly keeping quiet to avoid conflict).
- **Tilted to the Side:** This means a person is thoughtful or possibly considering what is being said.
- **Head High:** Holding the head high signals extreme confidence or feeling of superiority.
- **Chin Up:** The chin up indicates defiance, extreme confidence, or potentially arrogance.
- **Head Forward:** Head leaning forward indicates interest.
- **Head Tilted Down**: Tilting the head down signals disapproval, distrust, or potentially doubt.[12]

Eyebrows

One of the most natural indicators on a person's face is their eyebrows, which move subconsciously with a person's emotions. Like all body language indicators, they should be read as part of the entire package. Indicators to look for include:

- **Lowered:** Numerous meanings, including focus, consideration for what is being said, frustration, or anger.
- **Raised:** Surprise, directly correlated to the level of surprise (more surprise, higher raised eyebrows). Can also indicate openness.[13]

---

[12] https://www.tutorialspoint.com/body_language/body_language_head_positions.htm
[13] http://changingminds.org/techniques/body/parts_body_language/eyebrows_body_language.htm

Eyes

It's All in the Eyes

- **Peering to the Left:** Eyes in this direction can mean someone is remembering something or recollecting facts. Peering left and downward can indicate self-communication and looking left and to the side could mean an internal conversation is occurring.
- **Looking to the Right:** Looking to the right indicates imagination and can mean guessing or lying. If you combine looking right with looking down, it means there could be a self-question. On the other hand, if you combine looking right with looking up, it can mean lying.
- **Looking Sideways:** Looking sideways and to the right is associated with imagination. Looking sideways and to the left is potentially the exact opposite of imagination. In most cases, it means someone is accessing memory and remembering a story.
- **Direct Eye Contact:** When speaking, specifically in North America, this means sincerity and honesty. When listening, it indicates interest in the conversation at hand.
- **Wide Eyes:** The widening of the eyes or the furrowing of the brows (discussed later) signal wonder or surprise.
- **Rolling Eyes:** Rolling the eyes is a universal symbol of disbelief and possibly frustration. This can be viewed as hostile and rude.
- **Blinking:** Frequent blinking can indicate excitement. On the other hand, infrequent blinking could mean extreme boredom or extreme concentration, depending on focus. This is the perfect example of making sure, when reading body language, to take in the entire picture and not overfocus on one part.
- **Winking:** Winking is a friendly gesture or secret joke, possibly indicating mischief.
- **Rubbing Eyes:** Rubbing eyes may be caused by tiredness. It can also indicate disbelief or frustration.

Nose

Flaring: Can indicate frustration or displeasure.

Wrinking: Can indicate distasteful comment, not satisfied with own ideas.

Rubbing/Touching: Rubbing one's nose can indicate someone is not telling the truth or disagreement.[14]

---

[14] http://changingminds.org/techniques/body/parts_body_language/nose_body_language.htm

Mouth

The mouth is also a key indicator of body language. By reading the face, this can lead you to reading the full picture and supporting the initial indicators or changing your opinion based on additional information.

Turned Up/Down: Otherwise known as a smile or frown!

Pursed Lips: Disapproval/Distrust

Covering the Mouth: When this occurs, the person is literally embarrassed by the words coming out of their mouth so they cover it to conceal it. Could show embarrassment or distrust.

Lip Biting: Could be an indicator of nervousness or anxiousness.[15]

Facial Expressions

Facial expressions are an important part of body language and the first indicator of someone's mood. While some facial expressions are cultural, some are universal. Understanding the basics of facial expressions and decoding them will help you facilitate better communication.

Face = Emotion   Many studies that have concluded the universality of facial expressions have directly linked facial expressions to these emotions:

- **Happiness:** More than a smile is needed to indicate happiness. Genuine happiness should include the eyes. Eyelids can crinkle and when smiling wholesomely, the eyebrows naturally rise. (See Figure A.1.)
- **Anger:** A frown typically accompanies anger. Additionally, the eyes narrow, the chin points forward, and the eyebrows tend to furrow.
- **Fear:** Wide eyes and slightly raised eyebrows signal fear (similar to surprise, which can be hard to distinguish). The lips may be parted or stretched when the mouth is closed, as if the person is sucking in air due to the fear.
- **Surprise:** Surprise is similar to fear. The eyebrows become fully raised and the eyes are wide with surprise. The mouth is usually open. (See Figure A.2.)
- **Sadness:** The mouth turns down (frown) when someone is sad. A crease in the forehead and quivering chin accompany this slight frown, in addition to slightly furrowed eyebrows.

---

[15] https://www.verywellmind.com/understand-body-language-and-facial-expressions-4147228

FIGURE A.1 Happiness.

FIGURE A.2 Surprise.

FIGURE A.3 Disgust.

- **Disgust:** The expression of disgust includes the nose. The nose wrinkles or flares, the lips part, and the eyes narrow. (See Figure A.3.)

A flash of emotion will typically unconsciously appear on the face, even when attempting to keep one's feelings in check.

Hands

Tightly Clenched Hands: Can indicate someone under undue pressure. In many cases, people do this without realizing it when in a confrontation of conflict.

Standing and Joining Hands Behind Back: Superiority and authority.

Open Hands/Palms Up: Speaking with hands open usually means openness and trustworthiness.

Palms Down: Possibly indicates rigidity or defiance.

Rubbing Hands Together: Shows anticipation.

Clasping Hands/Squeezing Hands: Could mean someone is uncomfortable, nervous, or potentially scared.

Arms/Legs

Crossed Arms/Legs: Potentially signals defensiveness. This position is acting as a physical barrier to the person.

Open Arms/Extended: Openness and acceptance.

Feet

Pointing Toward: Feet pointing towards the other party usually shows interested in what is happening.

Tapping/Moving: Tapping feet can indicate impatience.

Gesture Clusters   Gestures are dependent on one another and together formulate a complete picture of what a person is thinking or seeing. In general, body language is as either being open or closed. Open body language can come from interest, confidence, aggression or even relaxation. Closed body language can be caused by defensiveness, the desire to hide or protect one's self or just simply being cold. Body language can be easy to read but can just as easily be misread.

Openness
- Open Hands/Posture
- Leaning Forward
- Uncrossed Legs/Arms
- Smiling

On the opposite end of the spectrum, open body language is just that: open. Legs not crossed, arms to one's side or used in conversation indicate interest and openness. Similar indications can be used with the hands. Open hands tend to keep the communication of body language open, in addition to everything we mentioned above.

Defensiveness
- Rigidity
- Arms/Legs Tightly Crossed
- Eyes Glancing/Darting Sideways
- Minimal Eye Contact
- Lips Pursed
- Fists Clenched
- Downcast Head

When objects or space is put in front of a person, it tends to be viewed as closed. Crossing your arms, sitting with your legs crossed and hunched forward is viewed as intensely closed off body language. Hands can be read as well. When in distress or conflict, your hands, when defensive or aggressive, tend to be balled up in fists or raised, as if to indicate to the other person to stop.

Please note: *It is essential to understand how people could misread your body language. If you are cold-natured, your body language could be read as defensiveness.*

Evaluation
- Tilted Head
- Hand to Cheek
- Leaning Forward
- Chin Stroking
- Eye squinted

Nervousness
- Clearing Throat
- Covering Mouth with Hand
- Tapping Fingers
- Whistling
- Jingling Pocket Change

- Fidgeting
- Twitching Lips/Face

We all have many unconscious gestures that can signal how we are feeling or what we are thinking. Nonverbal signals that are completely unconscious, such as very subtle shifts in the expression of the eyes or body positioning, are integral to understanding communication as these are impossible to fake. They are generated by thoughts and mental attitudes without our conscious volition or control.[16] Some unconscious gestures that many people have include:

- **Nail Biting:** This could indicate nervousness or insecurity.
- **Turning Away:** Looking away from someone that is speaking might indicate distrust/disbelief.
- **Pulling Ears:** Tugging at one's ears can indicate indecision.
- **Head Tilt:** A brief head tilt means interest. Holding a tilt could mean boredom or lack of understanding.
- **Open Palms:** Showing one's palms is a sign of innocence or sincerity.
- **Rubbing Hands Together:** Rubbing hands together is a sign of excitement or anticipation.
- **Touching the Chin:** This can indicate that a decision is being made or someone is considering what is being said.
- **Hand on the Cheek:** Touching their cheek can indicate someone is thinking.
- **Drumming of fingers:** This is a sign of impatience or boredom.
- **Touching one's Nose:** People often associate touching the nose with potentially lying. It can also signal doubt or rejection.

These are not only nervous ticks but can highlight the importance of understanding these.

Boredom/Impatience
- Drumming of Fingers
- Cupping the Head in the Palm of the Hand
- Foot Swinging
- Looking at a Watch Obsessively
- Turning One's Body and/or Peering at Exit

---

[16] https://www.alchemyassistant.com/topics/Ga2PExi7SUFMgjaD.html

Body Language Mistakes

Poor Posture

Posture can lead to unfair judgments and prejudices. Often, poor posture is seen as a closed body language that people assume is caused by a lack of confidence or defensiveness. There are, however, many different reasons why someone can have poor posture. Again, do not over-focus on one gesture or piece of body language.

Invading Personal Space

Depending on the cultures, the amount of personal space in a conversation can vary. There are general guidelines in Western society. Invading personal space is seen as an act of intimidation or potential hostility. There have been many studies on personal space zones, indicating four or five zones. Four zones generally used include[17]:

- **Intimate:** 0 to 24 inches. This space is reserved for intimate relationships, close friends, people that truly care for each other.
- **Personal:** 24 inches to 4 feet. Appropriate for private discussions between small parties.
- **Social:** Four to 12 feet. Appropriate for public and social conversations. Spacing is relatively open to allow others to join the conversation.
- **Public:** More than 12 feet. Routinely used for public speeches and important figures; assists in establishing authority.

Personal space can very significantly based on many different factors. Culture, background and situation could vary personal space greatly. At times, people will impede personal space to reiterate a key point or to come off aggressive or intimidating.

Communicating with Power

Communicating with power breeds confidence and respect. Some powerful movements that the team should consider:

- **Stance:** A wide stance with the feet apart indicates power. It is as simple as making yourself appear to be larger due to a wider stance. Hands on the hips with the elbows out (termed the "Superman Stance") take up space and indicates power.

---

[17] https://atworkjax.wordpress.com/2012/04/09/the-four-zones-of-interpersonal-space/

- **Walk:** Walk with a quick pace and take long strides tends to lean itself to powerful looking. Walking straight like previously mentioned, takes up more space and makes someone look bigger.

CHAPTER 10: PEOPLE-CENTRIC SKILLS

Remembering Names

There is a massive difference between hearing and listening. Hearing is a physical act that is natural and passive. Listening is a physical and mental process. To listen and remember a name, it has to be active and learned.

Active listening techniques show the person you are speaking to that you are listening. Take a piece of what was just stated and use it in your follow-up statement. Some **active listening techniques** include:

- Using encouraging words and reassuring sounds to convey interest ("I see.")
- Restating in your own words what the person said
- Repeating exactly what the person said ("Mirroring")
- Reflecting to show you understand how they feel ("You were pretty upset by this.")
- Probing the interviewee's initial response in order to expand and/or clarify the information given ("Please tell me more about that.")
- Summarizing ("These seem to be the main ideas you stated.")

Answering Questions That Sound Like an Attack

At some point, someone might ask a question that could be viewed as a borderline attack. What is the appropriate way to respond?

- Don't confront the person. Don't say, "No, I think you're wrong." There are many other ways to disagree with someone without saying, "I disagree." They will become defensive almost immediately.
- Affirm that their perspective is valid and appreciate the conversation. Do this by saying:
    - "That's an interesting point. Here's another way to look at it."
    - "I appreciate your thoughts. Let me give you a different perspective."
    - "I can see why you would have that opinion; here are my thoughts."

Everyone in the room will be interested to hear how you respond to the potential challenge. If you keep cool and say something positive before you deliver to your retort, they will be impressed with your professionalism and your command of the situation.

STARS Method to Quick Thinking
- **S**top and Breathe
- **T**ake Time to Listen
- **A**sk to Repeat the Question
- **R**epeat the Question Yourself
- **Si**lence Can Be Deafening

Stop and Breathe
- In order for your voice to remain calm and for your brain to "think," you have to be as *relaxed* as possible
- Take deep breaths (without being too obvious)
- Think positive
- Clench invisible muscles (thighs, biceps, feet) for a few seconds & release

Take Time to Listen
- Listening is the process of receiving, constructing meaning from, and responding to spoken and/or nonverbal messages; to hear something with thoughtful attention
- Effective communication is two-way
  - Dependent on speaking <u>and</u> listening
  - Email *should be* one-way communication

Ask to Repeat the Question
- Does this make you look unsure?
  - It makes you look concerned that you want to give an appropriate response. It also gives the questioner an opportunity to rephrase and ask a question that is more on point. Another opportunity to assess the intentions of the questioner
- If it is more specific or better worded, chances are the person really wants to learn more
- If the repeated question is more aggressive than the first one, then you know the person is more interested in making you uncomfortable than anything else

Repeat the Question Yourself
- Time to think & clarify exactly what is being asked
- It also allows you to rephrase (active listening) if necessary and put a positive spin on the request
- Ask for clarification
- Narrow the focus

Silence Can Be Deafening
- What does silence tell the speaker?

- It expertly communicates control (thoughts) and confidence in your answer expertly
- Rush to answer = Rush your words
- It also tells the speaker that you might need more information

CHAPTER 11: PEOPLE-CENTRIC SKILLS

The Feedback Sandwich

The Feedback sandwich is a method of introducing feedback to any employee by surrounding it with praise. It starts with the bread (positive feedback) to begin the conversation on a high note. Be careful not to spend too much time praising at the beginning, because the "meat" of the feedback message will be diluted.

Next, deliver the opportunity for growth in a positive tone. Avoid accusations but remain focused on the message that must be delivered. The "meat" should be the most tangible part of the conversation. Finally, close the feedback session on a positive note. Praise them on a strength they have or, in this instance, tell them you are confident they are going to adjust and be successful. This balances out the constructive feedback with some positivity.

The feedback sandwich can be overused. If an employee reacts negatively to the start of the conversation, shift into the feedback quickly. Be flexible in your approach to this conversation.

Providing Constructive Criticism

Providing constructive criticism is a skill that requires you to focus on four key areas:

1. **Focus on one issue at a time.** Avoid addressing multiple issues. This will only cause confusion and frustration.
2. **Focus on timely, specific feedback.** Once you identify an issue, make sure you do not wait too long to deliver the critique. The more time passes, the less affective it will be.
3. Most important, **focus on observable actions or behaviors**. Avoid generalities.
4. Finally, **focus on a plan to change the behavior.** Depending on the extent of change that must happen, your plan may be a simple adjustment."

Using Silence to your Advantage

Silence (when the other person is done speaking) shows (a) you are considering what is being said and (b) you expected more. More people will fill the silence and continue talking. After three to five seconds, end the silence (things will get awkward quickly).

 ## CHAPTER 12: PEOPLE-CENTRIC SKILLS

Crisis Management

- Understand the issue.
- What is the level of depth and breadth of the issue?
- How can we stop it?
- Do we need to publicly discuss?
- *Get ahead of the message.*

Which Is More Harmful?

- Coming out ahead of the message now, publicly (as much as possible) own-ing the message and sending the right message to the public: we will not tolerate unethical behavior.
     OR
- Taking the chance on news not leaking out and sending the wrong message internally, and not transparently communicating internally so the company becomes riddled with rumors and innuendo.

About the Author

Danny M. Goldberg is a well-known speaker on internal auditing and People-Centric Skills. Danny co-authored ***People-Centric Skills: Communication and Interpersonal Skills for Internal Auditors,*** via Wiley Publications. This is the first book published specifically to address the wide-ranging topic of communication skills for internal auditors. It has been offered through the IIA and ISACA bookstores since July 2015 and has sold over 4,000 copies (through 2019).

Danny is also accredited as the Professional Commentator of the Bureau of National Affairs, *Internal Audit: Fundamental Principles and Best Practices.* This book was authored by renowned audit scholars Curtis C. Verschoor and Mort A. Dittenhofer, co-author of *Sawyer's Internal Auditing.*

Danny has over 22 years of professional experience, including five years leading and building internal audit functions. He was named one of the Fort Worth Business Press 40 Under 40 for 2014 and he has published numerous articles in trade magazines. Danny has also published a children's book on communication skills, *Kid-Centric Skills,* available on Amazon.

Recognized as a top speaker at numerous conferences over the past ten years, Danny continues to speak, consult, and train as president and founder of GoldSRD, the Gold Standard in Staffing, Recruiting, and Professional Development.

Danny is a Certified Public Accountant, Certified Internal Auditor, Certified Information Systems Auditor, Certified in the Governance of Enterprise Information Technology, Certified in Risk and Information Systems Control, Certified in Risk Management Assurance, has obtained his Certification in Control Self-Assessment, and is a Chartered Global Management Accountant.

Danny is a very active member of the Institute of Internal Auditors (IIA), at both the local and national level. He has functioned in leadership roles at the IIA and with the American Lung Association and with local religious organizations. He has two kids: Caleb (12) and Liora (11). Danny is an avid reader writer and yoga enthusiast.

Index

Page numbers in *italic* denote a figure on the corresponding page.